Stories of the Gori
Narrated for You

Paul B. Du Chaillu

Alpha Editions

This edition published in 2024

ISBN : 9789362929983

Design and Setting By
Alpha Editions
www.alphaedis.com
Email - info@alphaedis.com

Contents

PRELIMINARY CHAPTER.

I had passed several years on the African Coast before I began the explorations recorded in my first book. In those years I hunted, traded with the natives, and made collections in natural history.

In such a wild country as Africa one does not go far without adventures. The traveller necessarily sees what is strange and wonderful, for everything is strange.

In this book I have attempted to relate some of the incidents of life in Africa for the reading of young folks. In doing this I have kept no chronological order, but have selected incidents and adventures here and there as they seem to be fitted for my purpose.

I have noticed that most intelligent boys like to read about the habits of wild animals, and the manners and way of life of savage men; and of such matters this book is composed. In it I have entered into more minute details concerning the life of the native inhabitants than I could in my other books, and have shown how the people build their houses, what are their amusements, how they hunt, fish, eat, travel, and live.

Whenever I am at a friend's house the children ask me to tell them something about Africa. I like children, and in this book have written especially for them. I hope to interest many who are yet too young to read my larger works.

CHAPTER II.

Some years ago a three-masted vessel took me to a wild country on the West Coast of Africa near the Equator.

It was a very wild country indeed.

As we came in sight of the land, which was coveredwith forest, canoes began to start from the shore towards us; and, as we neared the land, we could see the people crowding down on the beach to look at the strange sight of a vessel.

The canoes approached the vessel in great numbers. Some of them were so small that they looked like mere nutshells. Indeed, some of the men paddled with their feet; and one man carried his canoe ashore on his shoulder.

At last, the natives came on board, and what funny people they were! I could not discern one from another; they seemed to me all alike.

What a queer way of dressing they had too! You would have laughed to see them. Some had only an old coat on. Others had an old pair of trousers which probably had belonged to some sailor; these wore no shirt or coat. Some had only an old ragged shirt, and some again had nothing on except an old hat. Of course none of them had shoes.

How they shouted and hallooed as they came about the vessel! They seemed to speak such a strange language. No one on board appeared to understand them. They made so great a noise that I thought I should become deaf.

One of them had a fowl to sell; another brought an egg or two; and another a few bunches of plantains.

Our captain knew the coast; for he had long been an African trader, though he had never been at this place before.

The ship cast anchor. It was not far from a river called Benito.

I left the vessel and went ashore with some others. As I landed I was surrounded immediately by crowds of natives, who looked so wild and so savage that I thought they would kill me at once.

I was led to the village, which stood not far from the sea, and was hidden from view by the very large trees and the great forest that surrounded it. On one side of the village was a prairie.

I shall always remember this village. It was the first African village I had ever seen; and it was unlike those built in Southern Africa.

Don't think for a moment that I am going to speak to you of stone or wooden houses. No! These wild people lived in queer little huts, the walls of which were made of the bark of trees, and were not more than four or five feet high. The top of the roof was only about seven or eight feet from the ground. The length of these huts was about ten or twelve feet, and they were seven or eight feet wide. There were no windows, and the door was very small. They immediately took me to one of these houses, and said they gave it to me. They meant that it was mine as long as I would stay with them. It belonged to the son of the king.

So I went in. But where was I to sit down?

There was no chair to be seen.

Patience, thought I. These people had probably never seen a chair in their lives. It was so dark I could not see at first. By and by I saw how the hut was furnished. There were some calabashes to hold water, and two or three cooking pots. There were some ugly-looking spears, an axe, and two or three large and queer-looking knives, which could sever the head of a man at one blow. Of course I looked for a bed: I need not tell you there was none; but, instead, there were some sticks to lie upon. The very look of this sleeping-place made me shudder; I thought of snakes, scorpions, and centipedes. The dark hut seemed the very place for them. Shortly after the king's son came. If I remember well, his name was *Andèkè*. He told me that his father, the king, was ready to receive me.

The king ready to receive me!

This was a great announcement. I must dress.

But how?

There was no washing-basin to wash myself in; besides, I had forgotten my soap.

I was glad I had no beard at that time; for I do not know how I could have shaved.

In short, I resolved to go and see his majesty as I was.

The sun being very warm, I took my umbrella with me. The people conducted me to the royal palace.

What do you suppose a palace to be in the Benito country? The king's palace was made of the same material (bark of trees) as the houses I have just described to you; and it was only about twice as big.

As I entered I went towards the king, who was seated on a stool. Another empty stool was by his side.

I may say that Apourou—such was the king's name—did not come up to my ideas of a king. In fact, I should have laughed at him had I dared.

His costume was composed of a red soldier's coat, and he wore a little bit of calico round his waist. That was all. You must understand he had no shirt.

He was a tall, slim negro, with grey hair, and had large scars on his face, and his whole body was covered with tattoos. He wore large earrings. He was smoking a big ugly pipe.

He looked at me, and I looked at him.

The room was full of people, and the king had several of his wives around him. The queen was there. Would you believe it? in that country a man marries as many wives as he chooses!

The king looked at me for a long time without saying a word. Finally he opened his mouth, clapped his hands, and said I was a funny-looking *fellow*.

He next said he was very glad to see me, and would take care of me. Then he touched my hair, and said I must give him some. He would like to have me remain with him always. At this the people shouted, "We want the *ntangani* to stay with us!"

What do you think he did next?

He quietly proposed to me that I should get married to some of his countrywomen; and added that whomsoever I should choose would become my wife.

The suggestion was received by all the people with a tremendous grunt of approval, to show that they thought just as their king. Then they shouted, "The girl he likes he shall marry!"

I said, "I don't want to get married, I am too young." I did not want to tell him that I would not, for all the world, marry one of his people.

It was getting very warm in the hut, and there was a strong odour. The people were packed so closely together that they reminded one of herrings in a barrel, and you must remember I said the house had no windows.

Then the king presented me with one fowl, two eggs, and one bunch of plantain; and as I went away he said I had better give him my umbrella. But I went off as if I had not heard what he said. I thoughtit was rather too much for a king to ask a stranger to give up his umbrella. I had just begun to learn what African kings were.

The people followed me everywhere; I wish I could have understood their language. One man could talk English, and I am going now to give you a specimen of his English.

When he thought I must be hungry, he said, "Want chop? Want chop?" When he saw that I could not understand what he meant, he made signs with his hands and mouth, which at once explained to me that he had asked me if I wanted to eat. I said, "Yes;" and after a while, some cooked plantains, with some fish, were brought to me. I did not care for the plantains; it was the first time I had ever tasted them.

After my meal, I walked through the street of the village and came to a house, in the recess of which I saw an enormous idol. I had never in all my life seen such an ugly thing. It was a rude representation of some human being, of the size of life, and was made of wood. It had large copper eyes, and a tongue of iron, which shot out from its mouth to show that it could sting. The lips were painted red. It wore large iron earrings. Its head was ornamented with a feather cap. Most of the feathers were red, and came from the tails of grey parrots, while the body and face were painted red, white, and yellow. It was dressed in the skins of wild animals. Around it were scattered skins of tigers and serpents, and the bones and skulls of animals. Some food also was placed near, so that it might eat if it chose.

It was now sunset; and night soon set in over the village. For the first time in my life I stood alone in this dark world, surrounded by savages, without any white people near me. There was no light in the street, and only the reflection of the fires could be seen now and then. How dismal it was!

I looked at my pistols and my guns, and was glad to find that they were in good order.

By-and-by the people began to come out of their huts; and I saw some torches lighted, and taken towards the large *mbuiti* as they call the idol, and there placed on the ground. The large drums or tom-toms were also carried there; and the women and men of the village gathered around. The tom-toms beat; and, soon after, I heard the people singing. I went to see what was the matter.

What a sight met my eyes!

The men had their bodies painted in different colours. Some had one cheek red and the other white or yellow. A broad white or yellow stripe was painted across the middle of the chest and along both the arms. Others had their bodies spotted. Most ugly they looked! The women wore several iron or brass rings around their wrists and ankles.

Then the singing began, and the dancing! I had never seen such dancing before. It was very ungraceful. The drummers beat on the tom-toms with all their might. As they became warm with exertion their bodies shone like seals, so oily were they.

I looked and looked, with my eyes wide open; I was nearly stunned with the noise. As the women danced and sung, the brass and iron rings which they wore struck against each other, and kept time with the music and the beating of the tom-toms.

But why were they all there dancing and screeching around the idol?

I will tell you.

They were about to start on a hunting expedition, and they were asking the idol to give them good luck in their sport.

When I found it was to be a hunting expedition, I wanted to go at once with these savages, though I was only a lad under twenty years old.

I retired to my hut with a valiant heart; I was going to do great things.

If you had been in my place, boys, would you not have felt the same? Would you have left the gorillas alone? I am sure you all shout at once, "No! no!" Would you have let the elephants go unmolested in the forest? "Certainly not," will be your answer.

And what about the chimpanzee, and the big leopards who carry away so many people and eat them, the huge buffaloes, the wild boars, the antelopes, and the gazelles?

Would you have left the snakes alone?

Perhaps you are all going to say "Yes" to that; and I think you are right, for many of these snakes are very poisonous, and they are numerous in these great forests; for the country I am telling you about is nothing but an immense jungle. When a man is bitten by one of these snakes he often dies in a few minutes. There is also to be found in these woods an immense python, or boa, that swallows antelopes, gazelles, and many other animals. I shall have a good deal to tell you about them by-and-by.

So I resolved that I would try to see all these native tribes; that I would have a peep at the cannibals; that I would have a good look also at the dwarfs.

I am sure, that if any one of you had been with me on that coast, you would have said to me, "DuChaillu, let us go together and see all these things, and then come back home and tell the good folks all we have seen."

Yes, I am certain that every one of you would have felt as I did.

CHAPTER III.

A WEEK IN THE WOODS—A TORNADO—THE LEOPARDS PROWLING ABOUT—I KILL A COBRA AND A SCORPION— FIGHT WITH A BUFFALO—HUNTING FOR WILD BOARS—A LEOPARD TAKES A RIDE ON A BULL—SICK WITH THE FEVER.

Now, boys, fancy yourselves transported into the midst of a very dense and dark forest, where the trees never shed their leaves all at one time, where there is no food to be had, except what you can get with your gun, and where wild beasts prowl around you at night, while you sleep.

I found myself in such a place.

Immediately after we arrived in those gloomy solitudes we began to build an olako to shelter us from the rains.

I must tell you that Benito is a very strange country. It is situated, as you have seen by the map, near the equator. Of course, you know what the equator is? There, at a certain time of the year, the sun is directly above your head at noon, and hence it is the hottest part of the earth. The days and nights are of the same length. The sun rises at six o'clock in the morning, and the sunset takes place at six o'clock in the evening. There is only a difference of a few minutes all the year round. There is no twilight, and half an hour before sunrise or after sunset it is dark. There is no snow, except on very high mountains. There is no winter. There are only two seasons—the rainy season and the dry season. Our winter time at home is the time of the rainy season in Equatorial Africa, and it is also the hottest period of the year. It rains harder there than in any other country. No such rain is to be witnessed either in the United States or Europe. And as to the thunder and lightning! You never have heard or seen the like; it is enough to make the hair on your head stand on end. Then come the tornados, a kind of hurricane which, for a few minutes, blows with terrific violence, carrying before it great trees. How wild the sky looks! How awful to see the black clouds sweeping through the sky with fearful velocity!

So you will not wonder that we busied ourselves in preparing our shelter, for I remember well it was in the month of February. We took good care not to have big trees around us, for fear they might be hurled upon us by a tornado, and bury us all alive under their weight. Accordingly we built our olako near the banks of a beautiful little stream, so that we could get as much water as we wanted. Then we immediately began to fell trees. We carried two or three axes with us, for the axe is an indispensable article in the forests. With the foliage we made a shelter to keep off the rain.

While the men were busy building the olako, the women went in search of dried wood to cook our supper. We had brought some food from the village with us.

We were ready just in time. A most terrific tornado came upon us. The rain poured down in torrents. The thunder was stunning. The lightning flashed so vividly and often as nearly to blind us.

Our dogs had hidden themselves, indeed all animals and birds of the forest were much frightened, which was not to be wondered at. How thankful I was to be sheltered from such a storm! We had collected plenty of fuel, and our fires burned brightly.

We formed a strange group while seated around the fires, the men and women smoking their pipes and telling stories. We had several fires, and, as they blazed up, their glare was thrown out through the gloom of the forest, and filled it with fantastic shadows. Though tired, everybody seemed merry. We were full of hope for the morrow. Every one spoke of the particular animal he wished to kill, and of which he was most fond. Some wished for an antelope, others for an elephant, a wild boar, or a buffalo. I confess that I myself inclined towards the wild boar; and I believe that almost every one had the same wish, for that animal, when fat, is very good eating. Indeed, they already began to talk as if the pig were actually before them. All fancied they could eat a whole leg apiece, and their mouths fairly watered in thinking about it. No wonder they are so fond of meat, they have it so seldom. Who among us does not relish a good dinner, I should like to know?

By-and-by all became silent; one after the other we fell asleep, with the exception of two or three men who were to watch over the fires and keep them bright; for there were plenty of leopards prowling in theneighbouring forest, and none of us wanted to serve as a meal for them. In fact, before going to sleep, we heard some of these animals howling in the far distance. During the night, one came very near our camp. He went round and round; and, no doubt, lay in wait to see if one of us would go out alone; and then he would have pounced upon the careless fellow. I need not say we did not give him a chance; and you may be sure we kept the fire blazing. Finally, we fired a few guns, and he went off.

These leopards are dreadful animals, and eat a great many natives. They are generally shy; but once they have tasted human flesh, they become very fond of it, and the poor natives are carried off, one after another, in such numbers that the villages have to be abandoned.

The next day we went hunting. I had hardly gone into the forest when I saw, creeping on the ground under the dry leaves, an enormous black snake: I fancy I see it still. How close it was to me! One step more and I should have just trodden upon it, and then should have been bitten, and a few minutes after have died, and then, boys, you know I should have had nothing to tell you about Africa. This snake was a cobra of the black variety (*Dendrapspis angusticeps*). It is a very common snake in that region; and, as I have said, very poisonous.

As soon as the reptile saw me, he rose up, as if ready to spring upon me, gave one of his hissing sounds, and looked at me, showing, as he hissed, his sharp-pointed tongue. Of course, the first thing I did was to make a few steps backward. Then, levelling my gun, I fired and killed him. He was about eight feet long. I cut his head off, and examined his deadly fangs. What horrible things they were! They looked exactly like fish bones, with very sharp ends. I looked at them carefully, and saw that he could raise and lower them at will; while the teeth are firmly implanted in a pouch, or little bag, which contains the poison. I saw in the end of the fang a little hole, which communicated with the pouch. When the snake opens his mouth to bite, he raises his fangs. Then he strikes them into the flesh of the animal he bites, and brings a pressure on the pouch, and the poison comes out by the little hole I have spoken of.

I cut open the cobra, and found in his stomach a very large bird. Andèkè packed the bird and snake in leaves, and, on our return to the camp, the men were delighted. In the evening they made a nice soup of the snake, which they ate with great relish.

I had also killed a beautiful little striped squirrel, upon which I made my dinner. I felt almost sorry to kill it, it was such a pretty creature.

In the evening, as I was siting by the fire, and looking at the log that was burning, I spied a big ugly black scorpion coming out of one of the crevices. I immediately laid upon its back a little stick which I had in my hand. You should have seen how its long tail flew up and stung the piece of wood! I shuddered as I thought that it might have stung my feet or hands, instead of the wood. I immediately killed it, and the natives said these scorpions were quite common, and that people have to be careful when they handle dry sticks of wood, for these poisonous creatures delight to live under the dry bark, or between the crevices.

A nice country this to live in! thought I, after killing a snake and a scorpion the same day!

So when I lay down on my pillow, which was merely a piece of wood, I looked up to see if there was any scorpions upon it. I did not see any; but, during the night, I awoke suddenly and started up. I thought I felt hundreds of them creeping over me, and that one had just stung me, and caused me to wake up. The sweat covered my body. I looked around and saw nothing but sleeping people. There was no scorpion to be found. I must have been dreaming.

Not far from our camp was a beautiful little prairie. I had seen, during my rambles there, several footprints of wild buffaloes; so I immediately told Andèké we must go in chase of them. Andèké, the son of the king, was a very nice fellow, and was, besides, a good hunter—just the very man I wanted.

So we went towards the little prairie, and lay hidden on the borders of it, among the trees. By-and-by I spied a huge bull, who was perfectly unaware of my presence, for the wind blew from him to me; had the wind blown the other way, the animal would have scented me and made off. As it was, he came slowly towards me. I raised my gun and fired. My bullet struck a creeper, on its way, and glanced aside, so I only wounded the beast. Turning fiercely, he rushed at me in a furious manner, with his head down. I was scared; for I was, at that time, but a young hunter; I got ready to run, though I had a second barrel in reserve. I thought the infuriated bull was too powerful for me, he looked so big. Just as I was about to make my escape, I found my foot entangled and hopelessly caught in a tough and thorny creeper. The bull was dashing towards me with head down and eyes inflamed, tearing down brushwood and creepers, which barred his progress. Turning to meet the enemy, I felt my nerves suddenly grow firm as a rock. If I missed the bull all would be over with me. He would gore me to death. I took time to aim carefully, and then fired at his head. He gave one loud, hoarse bellow, and tumbled almost at my feet. In the meantime, Andèké was coming to the rescue.

I must say I felt very nervous after all was over. But being but a lad, I thought I had done pretty well. It was the first direct attack a wild beast had ever made upon me. I found afterwards, that the bulls are generally very dangerous when wounded.

Now I must tell you how this beast looked. He was one of the wild buffaloes frequently to be met with in this part of Africa. During the greater part of the day they hide in the forest. When much hunted they become very shy. They are generally found in herds of from ten to twenty-five, though I have found them sometimes in much greater number.

This animal (*Bos brachicheros*) is called by some of the natives "niaré." It is of the size of our cattle. It is covered with thin red hair, which is much darker in the bull than in the cow. The hoofs are long and sharp; the ears are fringed with most beautiful silky hair; the horns are very handsome, and bend backward in a graceful curve. In shape, the buffalo looks like something between an antelope and a common cow; and, when seen afar off, you might think these wild buffaloes were a herd of cattle at home.

How glad the people were when Andèké and I brought the news that we had killed a bull! There was great rejoicing. But I was tired and remained in the camp; while they went with knives and swords to cut the buffalo to pieces, and bring in the flesh.

What a fine place it was for hunting! The animals seemed to come down from the mountains beyond, and remain in the flat woody country along the seashore.

There were a great many wild boars. You know we all wanted one of these. So one night Andèké and I agreed to go and lie in wait for them on the prairie. In order to look like Andèké, I blackened my face andhands with charcoal, so that in the night the colour of my face could not be distinguished.

We started from the camp before dark, and reached the prairie before night. I stationed myself behind a large ant-hill not far from the open space. There I lay; one hour passed—two hours—three hours, and still neither wild boar nor buffaloes. I looked at Andèké. He was fast asleep, at the foot of another ant-hill close by. Once I saw a whole herd of gazelles pass by; but they were too far from me. Occasionally a grunt or the cracking of a twig, told me that a wild boar was not far off. At last everything became silent, and I fell asleep unconsciously.

Suddenly I was awakened by an unearthly roar—the yell of a wild beast.

I rubbed my eyes in a hurry—what could be the matter?

I looked round me, and saw nothing. The woods were still resounding with the cry that had startled me. Then I heard a great crash in the forest, made by some heavy animal running away. Then I saw emerge from the forest a wild bull, on whose neck crouched an immense leopard. The poor buffalo reared, tossed, roared and bellowed; but in vain. The leopard's enormous claws were firmly fixed in his victim's body, while his teeth were sunk deeply in the bull's neck. The leopard gave an awful roar, which seemed to make the earth shake. Then both buffalo and leopard disappeared in the forest, and the roars, and the crashing of the trees, soon ceased. All became silent again.

I had fired at the leopard, but it was too far off. We stayed a week here, and I enjoyed myself very much in the woods. I collected birds and butterflies, killed a few nice little quadrupeds, and then we returned to the seashore village. There the fever laid me low onmy bed of sickness. How wretched I felt! I had never had the fever before. For a few days my head was burning hot. When I got better, and looked at myself in my little looking-glass I could not recognise myself; I had not a particle of colour left in my cheeks and I looked as yellow and pale as a lemon. I got frightened. This fever was the forerunner of what I had to expect in these equatorial regions.

CHAPTER IV.

On the promontory called Cape St. John, about a degree north of the Equator stood a Mbinga village, whose chief was called Imonga. This was, I think, in the year 1852. The country around was very wild. The village stood on the top of a high hill which ran out into the sea, and formed thecape itself. The waves there beat with great violence against a rock of the tertiary formation. It was a grand sight to see those angry billows white with foam dashing against the shore. You could see that they were wearing away the rock. To land there safely was very difficult. There were only two or three places where between the rocks a canoe could reach the shore. The people were as wild as the country round them, and very warlike. They were great fishermen, and many of them spent their whole time fishing in their little canoes. Game being very scarce, there were but few hunters.

Imonga, the chief, had a hideous large scar on his face, which showed at once that he was a fighting man. Not a few of his men showed signs of wounds which they had received in battle. Many of these fights or quarrels took place in canoes on the water, among themselves, or with people of other villages.

I do not know why, but Imonga was very fond of me, and so also were his people. But one thing revolted me. I found that several of Imonga's wives had the first joint of their little finger cut off. Imonga did this to make them mind him; for he wanted his wives to obey him implicitly.

The woods around the village were full of leopards. They were the dread of the people, for they were constantly carrying off some one. At night, they would come into the villages on their errands of blood, while the villagers were asleep. There was not a dog nor a goat left; and within two months three people had been eaten by them; the very places could be seen in the huts where the leopards had entered. They would tear up the thin thatched palm leaves of the roofs, and having seized their victims, they would go back through the hole with a tremendous leap, and with the man in their jaws, and run off into the forest.

The last man taken uttered a piercing cry of anguish, which awoke all the villagers. They at once arose and came to the rescue, but it was too late. They only found traces of blood as they proceeded. The leopard had gone far into the woods, and there devoured his victim. Of course there was tremendous excitement, and they went into the forest in search of the leopard; but he could never be found. There were so many of these savage beasts that they even walked along the beach, not satisfied with the woods alone; and when the tide was low, during the night, the footprints of their large paws could be seen distinctly marked on the sand. After ten or eleven o'clock at night, no native could be seen on the seashore without torches.

During the day the leopard hides himself either in the hollow of some one of the gigantic trees, with which these forests abound, or sleeps quietly on some branch, waiting for the approach of night. He seldom goes out before one o'clock in the morning, unless pressed by hunger, and about four o'clock he goes back to his lair.

I was now getting accustomed to face danger. Killing the buffalo that attacked me had given me confidence.

To kill a leopard must be my next exploit.

I selected a spot very near the sands of the sea, where I remarked the leopards used to come every night, when the tide was low. I chose a day when the moon began to rise at midnight, so that it might not be so dark that I could not take a good aim at the leopard, and see what was going on.

I then began to build a kind of pen or fortress; and I can assure you I worked very hard at it. Every day I went into the forest and cut branches of trees, with which I made a strong palisade. Every stick wasabout six feet high, and was put in the ground about a foot deep. These posts were fastened together with strong creepers. My little fortress, for so I must call it, was about five feet square. This would never answer; for the leopard might leap inside and take hold of me. So with the help of some strong branches all tied strongly together I built a roof. Then I made loopholes on all sides for my guns, so that I might fire at the beast whenever he came in sight.

I was glad when I had finished, for I felt very tired. My axe was not sharp, and it had required several days to complete my work.

One clear starlight night, at about nine o'clock, I went and shut myself up in my fortress. I had taken a goat with me, which I tied a few yards from my place of concealment. It was quite dark. After I had tied the goat, I went back and shut myself very securely inside my stronghold.

I waited and waited, but no leopard came. The goat cried all the time. It was so dark that even if the leopard had come I could not have seen it.

The moon rose by one o'clock. It was in its last quarter; and very strange and fantastic it made everything look. There were the shadows of the tall trees thrown upon the white sand of the beach, while in the forest the gloom was somewhat greater. The sea came rolling on the beach in gentle waves, which, as they broke, sent up thousands of bright, phosphorescent flashes. There was a dead silence everywhere, except when the goat cried, or some wild beast made the forest resound with its dismal howl. The wind whispered gently, mournfully through the woods.

I could not account for it, but now and then a cold shudder ran through me. I was quite alone, for the negro I had taken with me was fast asleep.

One o'clock. No leopard. I looked in vain all round me: I could see nothing.

Two o'clock. Nothing yet.

Suddenly, I spied something a long way off on the beach, so far that I could not make out what it was. It came slowly towards me. What could it be? I asked myself. Soon I recognised a big spotted leopard. The goat, which had seen it, began to cry more loudly. The big beast came nearer and nearer. He began to crouch. Then he lay flat on the ground. How his eyes glittered! They looked like two pieces of bright, burning charcoal.

My heart beat. The first thought that came to me was—Is my house strong enough to resist his attack, in case I should wound him, or if, perchance, he should prefer me to the goat, and make an onslaught upon it?

The savage beast crawled nearer, and again crouched down on the ground. I took my gun; and, just as I was getting ready to fire, he made an immense leap, and bounded upon the goat. I fired. I do not know how, but, in the twinkling of an eye, the goat was seized, and both leopard and goat disappeared in the dark forest. I fired again, but with no better success. In the morning, I saw nothing but the traces of the poor goat's blood.

I did not return to the village till morning; for I dared not go outside of my palisade that night. So, the goat being gone, I concluded I had better light a fire, to warm myself, and drive away the mosquitoes. I always carried a box of matches with me. I struck one, and soon succeeded in making a blaze with the little firewood I had collected.

Strange enough I must have looked, inside of my cage, while the fire sent its glimmering light around.

Finally, seeing that everything was well secured, I went to sleep, taking good care to put myself in the middle of the fort, so that if, by any chance, a leopard came, he could not get hold of me with his paw. When I awoke it was broad daylight, and I immediately started for Imonga's village.

CHAPTER V.

THE BAY OF CORISCO—THE MANGROVE TREES—THE WONDERFUL FLOCKS OF BIRDS—WHAT I FOUND IN THE POUCH OF A PELICAN—HOW AN OLD KING IS BURIED, AND THE NEW KING CROWNED.

Now that you have followed me in the Benito country, and to Cape St. John, I will take you a little further down the coast to the Bay of Corisco. There, two rivers empty their waters into the sea. One of them is called the Muni river, and the other the Monda.

I will leave the Muni, for we shall have to come toit by-and-by, and will speak to you only of the Monda. It is throughout a low-banked swampy stream. The banks are covered with mangrove trees. Every limb or branch that grows in the water is covered with oysters—real oysters too; so that at low tide you can see, in some places for a long distance, immense beds of this kind of shell-fish.

The mangroves, on which the oysters grow so curiously, are very extraordinary trees. The main trunk, or parent tree, grows to an immense size. From a single tree a whole forest will grow up in time, for the branches send down shoots into the ground, which in their turn take root and become trees; so that, generally, almost the whole of the mangrove forest may be said to be knitted together.

The inhabitants of the country at the mouth of the river are called Shekiani. They are a very warlike tribe, and many of them are armed with guns, which they obtain from the vessels that come here from time to time to buy bar wood, ivory, or india-rubber.

I arrived at the mouth of the river, in a small canoe, manned by several Mbinga men. The canoe was made of the trunk of a single tree, and had a mat for a sail. At the mouth of the river, high above the swamps that surround its banks, are two hills. On the top of one of these hills, a village was situated. There I stayed. It was a village of insignificant size.

At low tide, the high muddy banks of the river are exposed. So many birds as are there, I never saw elsewhere: they are to be seen in countless thousands. The shore, the mud islands, and the water were so covered with them, that it was really a sight worth seeing. Here and there flocks of pelicans swam majestically along, keeping at a good distance from my canoe. You would probably wish to know what these pelicans are like. I will tell you. They are largebirds, and have an enormous bill, under which is a large pouch, capable of containing several pounds of fish. They have webbed feet, and their feathers are white. I wish you could see them looking out for their prey. How slyly they pry in the water for the fish they are in search of, and how quickly they pounce upon them unawares with their powerful beak! In an instant the fish are killed and stored away in the pouch; and when this is full, then Master Pelican begins to eat. The fish are put in the pouch as if it were a storehouse.

Now and then a string of flamingoes go stretching along the muddy shore, looking for all the world like a line of fire. Most beautiful are these flamingoes! and very singular they appear when not on the wing, but standing still on their long red legs! They are very wild, however, and difficult of approach.

Wherever the mud peeped out of the water, there were herons, cranes, gulls of various kinds. Scattered everywhere were seen those beautiful white birds (*Egretta flavirostris*). Some of the shore trees were covered with them, looking like snow in the distance.

Of course I wished to kill some of these birds. So I took a tiny little canoe, and covered it with branches of trees, that the birds might think it was a tree coming down the stream, as is often the case. Then I took a Shekiani with me to paddle, and, putting two guns in the canoe, we made for the pelicans. The sly birds seemed to suspect something, and did not give me a chance to approach them for a long time. But, as you know, in order to succeed in anything, people must have patience and perseverance. So, after chasing many, I finally succeeded in approaching one. He was just in the act of swallowing a big fish, when—bang!—I fired, and wounded him so that he could not fly. His wing had been broken by my shot. At the noise made by firing my gun, the birds flew away bythousands. I made for Master Pelican. The chase became exciting; but at last we succeeded in coming near him. But how to get hold of him was now the question. His wing only was broken; and, with his great beak, he might perhaps be able to cut one of my fingers right off. I was afraid to spoil his feathers if I fired again. He became exhausted, and with one of the paddles I gave him a tremendous blow on the head, which stunned him. Another blow finished him, and we lifted him into the canoe.

I cannot tell you how pleased I was. His pouch was full of fish. They were so fresh that I resolved to make a meal out of them.

I had hardly put the bird at the bottom of the canoe, when there came flying towards me a flock of at least two hundred flamingoes. In a moment I had my gun in readiness. Would they come near enough for me to get a shot at them? I watched them anxiously. Yes! Now they are near enough; and—bang! bang!—I fired the two barrels right into the middle of the flock, and two beautiful flamingoes fell into the water. Quickly we paddled towards them. In order to go faster I took a paddle also, and worked away as well as I could. They were dead. Both had received shots in the head.

We made for the shore. When I opened the pouch of the pelican—just think of it!—I found a dozen large fishes inside! They were quite fresh; and I am sure they had not been caught more than half an hour. You will agree with me that the pelican makes quick work when he goes a-fishing.

In the evening I felt so tired that I went straight to bed; and I slept so soundly, that if the Shekianis had chosen, they could have murdered me without my even opening my eyes.

This village had a new king; and I wondered if hismajesty were made king in the same fashion as the sovereign of the Mpongwe tribe; a tribe of negroes among whom I have resided, and I will tell you how their king was made.

Old King Glass died. He had been long ailing, but clung to life with determined tenacity. He was a disagreeable old heathen; but in his last days he became very devout—after his fashion. His idol was always freshly painted, and brightly decorated; his fetich, or "monda," was the best cared for fetich in Africa, and every few days some great doctors were brought down from the interior, and paid a large fee for advising the old king. He was afraid of witchcraft: he thought everybody wanted to put him out of the way by bewitching him. So the business of the doctors was to keep off the witches, and assure his majesty that he would live a long time. This assurance pleased him wonderfully, and he paid his doctors well.

The tribe had got tired of their king. They thought, indeed, that he was himself a most potent and evil-disposed wizard; and, though the matter was not openly talked about there were very few natives indeed who would pass his house after night, and none who could be tempted inside, by any slighter provocation than an irresistible glass of rum. In fact, if he had not been a great king, he would probably have been killed.

When he got sick at last, everybody seemed very sorry; but several of my friends told me in confidence, that the whole town hoped he would die; and die he did. I was awakened one morning, by those mournful cries and wails with which the African oftener covers a sham sorrow than expresses a real grief. All the women of the village seemed to be dissolved in tears. It is a most singular thing to see how readily the women of Africa can supply tears on the slightestoccasion, or for no occasion at all. They will cry together, at certain times of the day, on mourning occasions, when a few minutes before they were laughing. They need no pain or real grief to excite their tears. They can, apparently, weep at will.

The mourning and wailing on this occasion lasted six days. On the second day the old king was secretly buried, by a few of the most trusty men of the tribe, very early in the morning, before others were up; or perhaps at night. Some said he had been buried at night, while others said he had been buried in the morning, thus showing that they did not know. This custom arises from a belief that the other tribes would much like to get the head of the king, in order that with his brains they might make a powerful fetich.

During the days of mourning, the old men of the village busied themselves in choosing a new king. This, also, is a secret operation, and the result is not communicated to the people generally till the seventh day.

It happened that Njogoni (fowl), a good friend of mine, was elected. I do not know that Njogoni had the slightest suspicion of his elevation. At any rate, he shammed ignorance very well.

While he was walking on the shore, on the morning of the seventh day—probably some one had told him to go—he was suddenly set upon by the entire populace, who proceeded with a ceremony which is preliminary to the crowning. In a dense crowd they surrounded him, and then began to heap upon him every manner of abuse that the worst of mobs could imagine. Some spat in his face. Some beat him with their fists, not very hard of course. Some kicked him. Others threw dirty things at him. Those unlucky cues who stood on the outside and could only reach the poor fellow with their voices, assiduouslycursed him, and also his father, and especially his mother, as well as his sisters and brothers, and all his ancestors to the remotest generation. A stranger would not have given a farthing for the life of him who was presently to be crowned.

Amid the noise and struggle, I caught the words which explained all to me; for every few minutes some fellow, administering a comparatively severe blow or kick, would shout out, "You are not our king yet; for a little while we will do what we please with you. By-and-by we shall have to do your will."

Njogoni bore himself like a man, and a prospective king, and took all this abuse with a smiling face. When it had lasted about half an hour, they took him to the house of the old king. Here he was seated, and became again for a little while the victim of his people's curses and ill-usage.

Suddenly all became silent, and the elders of the people rose, and said solemnly (the people repeating after them), "Now we choose you for our king; we engage to listen to you, and to obey you."

Then there was silence; and presently the silk hat, of "stove-pipe" fashion, which is the emblem of royalty among the Mpongwe and several other tribes, was brought in, and placed on Njogoni's head. He was then dressed in a red gown, and received the greatest marks of respect from all those who had just now abused him.

Then followed six days of festival, during which the poor king, who had taken the name of his predecessor, was obliged to receive his subjects in his own house, and was not allowed to stir out. The whole time was occupied in indescribable gorging of food, and drinking of bad rum and palm wine. It was a scene of beastly gluttony and drunkenness and uproarious confusion. Strangers came from the surrounding villages. Everything to eatand drink was furnished freely, and all comers were welcome.

Old King Glass, for whom during six days no end of tears had been shed, was now forgotten; and *new* King Glass, poor fellow, was sick with exhaustion.

Finally, the rum and palm wine were drank up, the food was eaten, the allotted days of rejoicing had expired, and the people went back to their homes.

CHAPTER VI.

AN OLD MAN KILLED FOR WITCHCRAFT—MY JOURNEY TO THE COUNTRY OF THE CANNIBALS—STARTING ON THE ROUTE.

In the year 1856 I was again in the equatorial regions. I was in the great forest, on my way to the cannibal country; yes, the country where the people eat one another. It was a long way off, and how was I to get there through the dense jungle? How was I to find my way in that vastAfrican forest? These were the thoughts that troubled me when I was in the village of Dayoko.

The village of Dayoko lies not far from the banks of the Ntambounay river, and is surrounded by beautiful groves of plantain trees.

Dayoko is one of the chiefs of the Mbousha tribe, and a wild and savage set of people they are I can tell you. But Dayoko became my friend, and said he would spare me a few men to take me part of the way.

These Mbousha people look very much like the Shekiani I have already described. They are superstitious and cruel, and believe in witchcraft. I stayed among them only a few days. I will now tell you what I saw there.

In a hut I found a very old man. His wool (hair) was white as snow, his face was wrinkled, and his limbs were shrunken. His hands were tied behind him, and his feet were placed in a rude kind of stocks. Several negroes, armed to the teeth, stood guard over him, and now and then insulted him by angry words and blows, to which he submitted in silence. What do you suppose all this meant?

This old man was to be killed for witchcraft!

A truly horrible delusion this witchcraft is!

I went to Dayoko, the chief, to try to save the old man's life, but I saw it was in vain.

During the whole night I could hear singing all over the town as well as a great uproar. Evidently they were preparing for the sacrifice of the old man.

Early in the morning the people gathered together with the fetich-man. His blood-shot eyes glared in savage excitement, as he went around from man to man. In his hands he held a bundle of herbs with which he sprinkled, three times, those to whom hespoke. Meantime, there was a man on the top of a high tree close by, who shouted, from time to time, "Jocou! Jocou!" at the same time shaking the trees.

"*Jocou*" means "devil" among the Mbousha; and the business of this man was to scare the evil spirit, and keep it away.

At last they all declared that the old man was a most potent wizard, that he had killed many people by sorcery, and that he must be killed.

You would like to know, I dare say, what these Africans mean by a wizard, or a witch? They believe that people have, within themselves, the power of killing anyone who displeases them. They believe that no one dies unless some one has bewitched him. Have you ever heard of such a horrible superstition? Hence those who are condemned for witchcraft are sometimes subjected to a very painful death; they are burnt by slow fire, and their bodies are given to the Bashikouay ant to be devoured. I shall have something to tell you about ants by-and-by. The poor wretches are cut into pieces; gashes are made over their bodies and cayenne pepper is put into the wounds. Indeed it makes me shudder to think of it, for I have witnessed such dreadful deaths, and seen many of the mutilated corpses.

After I witnessed the ceremony, the people scattered, and I went into my hut, for I was not well. After a while I thought I saw a man pass my door, almost like a flash, and after him rushed a horde of silent but infuriated men towards the river. In a little while, I heard sharp, piercing cries, as of a man in great agony, and then all became still as death.

I came out, and going towards the river was met by the crowd returning, every man armed, with axe, spear, knife or cutlass; and these weapons, as well as their own hands, and arms, and bodies were sprinkled with blood.

They had killed the poor old man they called a wizard, hacked him to pieces, and finished by splitting open his skull, and scattering the brains into the water. Then they returned. At night these blood-thirsty men seemed to be as gentle as lambs, and as cheerful as if nothing had happened.

Ought we not to be thankful that we were born in a civilized country?

Now came the "grand palaver" over my departure. I called Dayoko and all the elders of the village together. When they had all assembled, I told them I must go into the Fan country inhabited by the cannibals.

Dayoko said I should be murdered by the cannibals, and eaten up, and tried to dissuade me from going.

Finally I said that go I would.

So it was determined that I should go under Dayoko's protection. Accordingly he gave me two of his sons to accompany me, and ordered several men to carry my chests, guns, powder, bullets, and shot. They were to take me to one of Dayoko's fathers-in-law, a Mbondemo chief who lived in the mountains.

I was going farther and farther from the sea; if the savages were to leave me and run away in the forest, what would become of me?

We started in canoes, ascended the Muni river, and then paddled up the river called the Ntambounay (you must not mind these hard names, they are not of my choice. I must call things by the names the natives give them).

After paddling all day, towards sunset we all felt very tired; for we had gone a long way up the river, and reached a Shekiani village. I was quite astonished to meet Shekiani here, but so it happened.

I shall always remember this Shekiani village, for I thought I should be murdered and plundered there. After we had landed in the village, I was told at once, that I could not go any further, for the road belonged to them. I must pay a tribute of six shirts similar to those I wore, three great-coats, beads, etc., etc. This would have entirely ruined me.

I could not sleep at all. Through the whole night a crowd surrounded my hut, talking, shouting, and singing in the greatest excitement. My guns and revolvers were all loaded and I made up my mind not to be killed without fighting desperately. If I was to die, I resolved at all events to die like a brave man. All my party were in my hut except Dayoko's two sons, who had gone to talk with the Shekiani chief. The Shekiani chief was a friend of Dayoko, and Dayoko's sons told him I was their father's stranger-friend.

At last, things became more quiet; and, towards morning, the people were still or asleep.

We left the hut. All was still peaceful. My men said that Dayoko's sons had a big fetich to avert war.

I gave a present to the Shekiani chief, and off we started. We left our large canoes and took smaller ones; for we were to go through a very small stream.

As we ascended the beautiful river, we could see the lofty mountains of the interior. A great many islands studded the stream. From the trees on the banks, the monkeys looked down at us with astonishment. What curious creatures they were, with their black faces peeping out through the dark foliage, and looking as if they were making grimaces at us. By-and-by we left the river and made our way along the creeks or through the woods towards the Mbondemo village. Now and then we walked freely through the wide openingswhich the elephants had made. The rushing of a herd of elephants effects quite a clearing in the forest. On we went, till finally we came to a place where a great number of large trees had been prostrated. Wherever we looked, trees were lying on the ground, many of them of enormous size. As I looked I heard, not far off, a tremendous crash—a most awful noise. I could not conjecture what was the matter. It turned out that a tree had come down; and as it fell, being a huge one, it crushed a dozen others around it, and each as it broke gave a great crash, so that the combined effect was awful to hear.

We had to go through these fallen trees; and what tough work it was! I never had seen anything like it. Now we had to climb on a fallen tree and follow its trunk; then we had to come down, and were entangled in its branches or in those of other trees. At other times we had to creep under them. I was continually afraid that my gun would be fired off by some creepers or boughs getting hold of the trigger.

At last, when my patience was entirely gone, and my few clothes literally hanging in ribbons about me, my legs sadly wounded, and my face and hands scratched, we arrived at the camp of the Mbondemos, situated almost at the foot of the mountain.

These mountains were covered with an immense forest; and so thick were the trees that no open view could be obtained in any direction. The mountains ended somewhere in the interior, no one knew where, but this they knew, that it was near the home of the Fans, a cannibal tribe, and that elephants were plentiful, and gorillas were occasionally seen there. This encampment of the Mbondemos was called an Olako. There was not a house in the camp, and it was a romantic scene to look at. Scattered under huge trees, on the edge of the woods, were leafy shelters, openingtowards the forest. Under these the people lived. A few sticks put close together formed their beds. They contrived to sleep upon them, and I did the same. I assure you that they were hard enough, and reminded me that a mattress was a very good thing. Every family had its fire prepared beside the beds; and around these fires in the evening they clustered, men, women, and children.

The chief of this Mbondemo encampment was called Mbéné, and I liked him very much. He was very kind to me, and always tried to furnish me with food. There was scarcity of provisions, at the time, in the camp of the Mbondemos. There were no plantain and cassada fields near, and often I had to go without breakfast or dinner. The people lived chiefly on the nuts of the forest, and at that season of the year these were very scarce.

Poor Mbéné said they had very little to eat, but would give me what they could. I had carried with me a few little crackers, which I found very precious, more precious than gold, and which I reserved for time of sickness; but one by one they disappeared. I looked at them every time I took one; but I felt so hungry that I could not refrain from eating them.

Have you known what hunger is—real craving hunger? I can assure you it is a dreadful feeling.

During that time of the year, this people had half the time nothing to eat but the nut of a kind of palm.

This nut was so bitter I could scarcely eat it. It is shaped like an egg, with rounded ends. To prepare it for eating, it is divested of its husk, and soaked in water for twenty-four hours, when it loses part of its exceedingly bitter taste, and becomes tolerably palatable, that is, to a starving man. Sometimes hunger willmake them eat the nut without soaking it. I have done so myself, when lost in the forest. It is dreadfully disagreeable.

Now and then, the women succeeded in getting a few little fish in the streams, and gave me some. I could bear a good deal, for I had firmly resolved to go into the cannibal country.

These Mbondemos are continually moving their villages. Mbéné has moved his village three times within a few years. I asked him why he made these frequent changes. He said he moved the first time because a man had died, and the place was "not good" after that event. The second time he was forced to move because they had cut down all the palm trees, and would get no more mimbo (palm wine), a beverage of which they are excessively fond. They tap the palm, just as the maple tree is tapped in America, only they tap the tree at the top. This palm wine has somewhat of a milky colour; and, when drunk in great quantity, it intoxicates. The palm trees are very plentiful all over this part of the country, and it seems easier for them to move than to take care of the trees surrounding their settlements, useful as they are to them; for they furnish not only the wine they love, but the bitter nut I mentioned before, which often keeps them from actual starvation. When the tree is cut down they get what we call the palm cabbage which grows at the top. When cooked this palm cabbage is very good.A country which has plenty of palm trees, plenty of game, a good river or rivulet, and plenty of fish, is the country for a Mbondemo settler or squatter.In these forests there is a vine or creeper which I might call the traveller's vine. If thirsty you may cut it, and within less than a minute a tumblerful of waterwill come out of it. This vine hangs about in the forest, and seemed to me to grow without leaves. What a capital thing it would be if water were not abundant in this country! The water procured from it has hardly any taste, and is perfectly pure and limpid.

Being unable to endure the continual hunger, I called Mbéné, and told him that his place had no food to give, and he must take me to a country where there was something to eat, and which would be on my way to the Fan country. Good Mbéné said, "Spirit, I will try the best I can to take you where you want to go. I will send some of my people with you."

In the meantime, Dayoko's people had all returned to their village. These forests had no game. I spent hour after hour scouring the forest, but I could see nothing, except birds, some of which were extremely pretty. I am afraid that if I had succeeded in killing a snake I should have eaten it, as I felt desperately hungry. I did not like the bitter nuts; so it was agreed that Mbéné's brother Mcomo, together with several of his people, should accompany me as far as the country of the Fan tribe. I could hardly believe such good news to be true.

Mbéné's wife always cooked my food. She was a dear good old woman, and I gave her a fine necklace of beads when I left. She was delighted with my present. They were big white porcelain beads of the size of a pigeon's egg. One day Mbéné succeeded in getting a fowl for me. His wife cooked it; she made soup, and put plenty of cayenne pepper into it. I had also some plantain. How I enjoyed this meal! the more so that it was probably the last I should get for a good many days, unless we were unusually lucky, and should kill some antelopes or elephants on our road to the Fan country.

Elephant meat is execrable, as you would say on tasting it. But as you may not have the chance I will tell you by-and-by how it tastes.

As much food as possible was collected for our journey, and at last everything was ready.

CHAPTER VII.

OUR JOURNEY THROUGH THE WILDERNESS CONTINUED—A REBELLION IN CAMP—NOTHING TO EAT—I SHOOT A FISH AND MISS AN ELEPHANT—I KILL A BIG SNAKE, AND THE OTHERS EAT HIM—MY FIRST SIGHT OF GORILLAS.

Before we renewed our journey the natives had done all they could to gather provisions; but the result was poor enough. By going to distant villages they had succeeded in getting a few bunches of plantain.

Mcomo, Mbéné's brother, backed out. He said he was not going into the cannibal country to be eaten up. But I must tell you that Mbéné had some friends among the cannibals. And he sent with me two of his sons called Miengai and Makinda, together with twelve good hunters, and six women who were the wives of some of the men. The women carried the provisions, etc.

I took seventy pounds of shot and bullets, nineteen pounds of powder, ten pounds of arsenic for preserving the birds and animals I should kill, for I knew I should probably succeed in getting some new specimens.

When all was arranged, when everybody had taken leave of all his friends, for this was a very great journey, and they came back half-a-dozen times to take leave over again, or say something they had forgotten, when all the shouting and quarrelling about who should carry the smallest load was over, we at last got away.

We had left the camp of Mbéné behind us at a distance of about five miles when we came to the banks of a little river called the Noonday, a clear and beautiful stream. I was ahead of the party with Miengai, and was waiting for the others to come up before crossing. As we stood on the banks I spied a fish swimming along. Immediately the thought came into my mind, "How nicely that fish would taste if I could get it and boil it in a pot over the fire!" I fired a charge of small shot into it; but no sooner had I pulled the trigger than I heard a tremendous crash on the opposite bank about six or seven yards off. Small trees were torn down violently, and then we heard the shrill trumpetings of a party of frightened elephants. They were probably sleeping or standing in a dead silence on the opposite bank in the jungle. I was sorry I had fired, for after crossing the stream we might have killed an elephant. Poor Miengai was terribly vexed. "I am sure," said he, "they had big tusks of ivory."

Our party, as soon as they heard the gun, came up in haste, and asked what was the matter. When they heard the story they began to lament our not killing an elephant; for then we should have had meat enough for the whole journey; and they shouted with one accord: "Elephant meat is so good!"

This exclamation made me wonder how an elephant steak would taste.

On we went, and got fairly into the mountainous country. The hills became steeper as we advanced. How tired I felt; for the diet at Mbéné's camp had not strengthened me. These Mbondemos had a great advantage over me. They used their bare feet almost as deftly as monkeys, and hence got their foothold more easily than I.

Miengai and I were in advance. All at once he made me a sign to keep very still. I thought he had discovered a herd of elephants, or seen the traces of an enormous leopard. He cocked his gun; I cocked mine; the other men did the same; and there we stood in perfect silence, for at least five minutes. Suddenly Miengai sent a "hurrah" echoing through the forest. It was immediately answered by shouts from many voices not very far off, but whose owners were hidden from us by huge rocks and trees. Miengai replied with the fierce shout of the Mbondemo warriors, and was again answered. Thinking we were going to have a general fight, I looked carefully after my powder flask and my bullets, and found they were all right. Going a little farther on, we came in sight of the encampment of a large party, who proved to be some of Mbéné's people just returning from a trading expedition to the interior. Two men of this camp offered to go with us. Their names were Ngolai and Yeava. We consented to take them.

What a journey it was! Nothing but thick woods to struggle through, hills to climb, rivers to cross, and nearly all the time it rained; in fact, I was wet from morning to night. How glad I was when, in the evening, we had made our camp, and built great fires!For my part, I had three fires lit about my bed of leaves; and in the evening I always hung up my clothes to dry, so as to have them ready for the next day.

One morning my men came to tell me they were tired, and would not go a step farther unless I gave them more cloth.

They seemed in earnest; and I began to question myself whether they meant to plunder me or to leave me in these mountains. To be left thus alone would have been almost certain death. To give them what they asked was to show them I was afraid of them. If they knew I was afraid of them I did not know what they might next do. So I determined to put on a bold front. Taking my two revolvers in my hand, I said: "I will not give you any more cloth. I will not let you leave me, because your father Mbéné has given you to me to accompany me to the Fan tribe. You must therefore go with me, or" (here I motioned with my pistols) "there will be war between us. But," said I, "this is a very hard road, and at the end of the journey I will give you something more."

This satisfied them, and we again resumed our journey. Up, and up, and up we struggled, and now we began to meet with immense boulders. Not the scream of a bird, or the shrill cry of a monkey, broke the stillness of the dark solitude. Nothing was heard but the panting breaths of our party as we ascended the hills.

At last we came to an immense mountain torrent, which rushed down the hillside with fearful force, and was white with foam. Its course was full of huge granite boulders, which lay about as though the Titans had been playing at skittles in that country. Against these the angry waters dashed as if they would carryall before them, and, breaking, threw the milky spray up to the very tree-tops. As I looked up the torrent seemed to pour its foaming waters directly down upon us.

This was the head of the Ntambounay river which I had ascended in a canoe, and on the banks of which I came near being murdered in the Shekiani village. What a change had taken place in it! Here a canoe would be dashed into a hundred pieces against the rocks.

I was so thirsty and tired that I went to the river's bank, and drank a few handfuls of the pure, clean cold water.

After resting a little while, we continued our course till we reached the top of a very high mountain, whence I could see all the country round. How wild and desolate it looked! Nothing but forest and mountains stretching away as far as the eye could reach.

I was sitting under a very large tree, when, suddenly looking up, I saw an immense serpent coiled upon the branch of a tree just above me; and I really could not tell whether he was not about to spring upon me and entangle me in his huge folds. You may well believe that I very quickly "stood from under." I rushed out, and taking good aim with my gun, I shot my black friend in the head. He let go his hold, tumbled down with great force, and after writhing convulsively for a time, he lay before me dead. He measured thirteen feet in length, and his ugly fangs proved that he was venomous.

My men cut off the head of the snake, and divided the body into as many pieces as there were people. Then they lighted a fire, and roasted and ate it on the spot. They offered me a piece; but, though very hungry, I declined. When the snake was eaten I was the only individual of the company that had an empty stomach; I could not help reflecting on the disadvantage it is sometimes to have been born and bred in a civilized country, where snakes are not accounted good eating.

We now began to look about the ruins of the village near which we sat. A degenerate kind of sugar-cane was growing on the very spot where the houses had formerly stood. I made haste to pluck some of this, and chew it for the little sweetness it had. While thus engaged my men perceived what instantly threw us all into the greatest excitement. Here and there the cane was beaten down or torn up by the roots; and, lying about, were fragments which had evidently been chewed. There were also footprints to be seen, which looked almost like those of human beings. What could this mean? My men looked at each other in silence, and muttered, "Nguyla!" (Gorillas!).

It was the first time I had seen the footprints of these wild men of the woods, and I cannot tell you how I felt. Here was I now, it seemed, on the point of meeting, face to face, that monster, of whose ferocity, strength, and cunning the natives had told me so much, and which no white man before had hunted. My heart beat till I feared its loud pulsations would alarm the gorilla. I wondered how they looked. I thought of what Hanno the Carthaginian navigator said about the wild hairy men he had met on the West Coast of Africa more than two thousand years ago.

By the tracks it was easy to know that there must have been several gorillas in company. We prepared at once to follow them.

The women were terrified. They thought their end had come—that the gorilla would be soon upon them. So, before starting in search of the monster, we left two or three men to take care of them and reassure them. Then the rest of us looked once more carefullyat our guns; for the gorilla gives you no time to reload, and woe to him whom he attacks! We were fortunately armed to the teeth.

My men were remarkably silent, for they were going on an expedition of more than usual risk; for the male gorilla is literally the king of the forest—the king of the equatorial regions. He and the crested lion of Mount Atlas are the two fiercest and strongest beasts of that continent. The lion of South Africa cannot be compared with either for strength or courage.

As we left the camp, the men and women left behind crowded together, with fear written on their faces. Miengai, Ngolai, and Makinda set out for the hunt in one party; myself and Yeava formed another. We determined to keep near each other; so that in case of trouble, or in a great emergency, we might be at hand to help one another. For the rest, silence and a sure aim were the only cautions to be given.

As we followed the footprints, we could easily see that there were four or five of them, though none appeared very large. We saw where the gorillas had run along on all fours, which is their usual mode of progression. We could perceive also where, from time to time, they had seated themselves to chew the canes they had borne off. The chase began to be very exciting.

We had agreed to return to the women and their guards and consult about what was to be done, after we had discovered the probable course of the gorilla; and this was now done. To make sure of not alarming our prey, we moved the whole party forward a little way, to some leafy huts, built by passing traders, and which served us for shelter and concealment. Here we bestowed the women, whose lively fear of the terrible gorilla arises from various stories current among the tribes, of women having been carried off into thewoods by the fierce animal. Then we prepared once more to set out on our chase, this time hopeful to get a shot.

Looking once more to our guns, we started off. I confess that I was never more excited in my life. For years I had heard of the terrible roar of the gorilla, of its vast strength, of its fierce courage when only wounded. I knew that we were about to pit ourselves against an animal which even the enormously large leopards of the mountains fear, which the elephants let alone, and which perhaps has driven away the lion out of this territory; for the "king of beasts," so numerous elsewhere in Africa, is not met with in the land of the gorilla.

We descended a hill, crossed a stream on a fallen log, crept under the trees, and presently approached some huge boulders of granite. In the stream we had crossed we could see plainly signs that the animals had just crossed it, for the water was still disturbed. Our eyes wandered everywhere to get a glimpse of our prey. Alongside of the granite blocks lay an immense dead tree, and about this the gorillas were likely to be.

Our approach was very cautious; I wish you could have seen us. We were divided into two parties. Makinda led one, and I the other. We were to surround the granite block, behind which Makinda supposed the gorillas to be hiding. With guns cocked and ready we advanced through the dense wood, which cast a gloom, even in midday, over the whole scene. I looked at my men, and saw that they were even more excited than myself.

Slowly we pressed on through the dense bush, dreading almost to breathe, for fear of alarming the beasts. Makinda was to go to the right of the rock, while I took the left. Unfortunately he and his party circled it at too great a distance. The watchful animals sawhim. Suddenly I was startled by a strange, discordant, half human, devilish cry, and beheld four young and half-grown gorillas running towards the deep forest. I was not ready. We fired, but hit nothing. Then we rushed on in pursuit; but they knew the woods better than we. Once I caught a glimpse of one of the animals again; but an intervening tree spoiled my mark, and I did not fire. We pursued them till we were exhausted, but in vain. The alert beasts made good their escape. When we could pursue no more we returned slowly to our camp, where the women were anxiously expecting us.

I protest I felt almost like a murderer when I saw the gorilla this first time. As they ran on their hind legs, with their heads down, their bodies inclined forward, their whole appearance was that of hairy men running for their lives. Add to all this their cry, so awful, yet with something human in its discordance, and you will cease to wonder that the natives have the wildest superstitions about these "wild men of the woods."

In our absence the women had made large fires, and prepared the camp. I changed my clothes, which had become drenched by the frequent torrents and puddles we ran through in our eager pursuit. Then we sat down to our supper, which had been cooked in the meantime. I noticed that all my plantains were gone—eaten up. What was to become of us in the great forest? I had only two or three biscuits, which I kept in case of actual starvation or sickness.

As we lay by the fire in the evening before going to sleep, the adventure of the day was talked over to those who had not gone with us; and, of course, there followed some curious stories of the gorillas. I listened in silence.

One of the men told a story of two Mbondemo women who were walking together through the woods, when suddenly an immense gorilla stepped into the path, and, clutching one of the women, bore her off in spite of the screams and struggles of both. The other woman returned to the village much frightened, and told the story. Of course her companion was given up for lost. Great was the surprise when, a few days afterwards, she returned to her home.

"Yes," said one of the men, "that was a gorilla inhabited by a spirit." This explanation was received by a general grunt of approval.

One of the men told how, some years ago, a party of gorillas were found in a cane-field tying up the sugar-cane in regular bundles, preparatory to carrying it away. The natives attacked them, but were routed, and several killed, while others were carried off prisoners by the gorillas; but in a few days they returned home, not uninjured indeed, for the nails of their fingers and toes had been torn off by their captors.

Then several people spoke up, and mentioned names of dead men whose spirits were known to be dwelling in gorillas.

Finally came the story that is current among all the tribes who are acquainted with the habits of the gorilla, that this animal will hide himself in the lower branches of a tree, and there lie in wait for people who go to and fro. When one passes sufficiently near, the gorilla grasps the luckless fellow with his powerful feet, which he uses like giants' hands, and, drawing the man up in to the tree, he quietly chokes him there.

Hunger and starvation began to tell upon us severely. When we started I did not calculate on meeting with gorillas. I had eaten all my sea bread. There was not a particle of food among us, and no settlement near us. I began to feel anxious for fear that we should die. Berries were scarce; and nuts werehardly to be found. The forest seemed deserted. There was not even a bird to kill. To make matters worse, we had been misled. We were lost—lost in the great forest!—and we failed to reach a certain settlement where we had expected to arrive.

Travelling on an empty stomach is too exhausting to be very long endured. The third day I awoke feeble, but found that one of the men had killed a monkey. This animal, roughly roasted on the coals, tasted delicious. How I wished we had ten monkeys to eat! but how glad and grateful we were for that single one.

Presently, Makinda, looking up, discovered a beehive. He smoked the bees out, and I divided the honey. There might have been a fight over this sweet booty had I not interposed and distributed it in equal shares. Serving myself with a portion not bigger than I gave the rest, I at once sat down, and devoured honey, wax, dead bees, worms, dirt, and all; I was so hungry. I was only sorry we had not more.

I had really a hard time getting through the old elephant tracks, which were the best roads through the jungle. The men seemed to have lost their way. We saw no animals, but found several gorillas' tracks.

At last my men began to talk more cheerfully; they knew where they were: and, soon after, I saw the broad leaves of the plantain, the forerunner of an African town. But, alas! as we approached, we saw no one coming to meet us; and when we reached the place we found only a deserted village. But even for this how thankful I was! Since I left Dayoko I had experienced nothing but hunger and starvation; and these were the first human habitations we had met.

Presently, however, some Mbicho people made their appearance. They were relatives of Mbéné, and their village was close by. They gave us some plantains, but no fowls. I wished very much to get a fowl. I feltgouamba (which means hunger) for meat, and knew that a good warm fowl broth would have done me a great deal of good. We spent the evening in the houses, drying and warming ourselves. It was much better than the forest, even if it was only a deserted town.

I asked if we should ever reach the cannibal country, and found that, with the exception of the Mbicho village near at hand, we were already surrounded on three sides by Fan villages.

I was too tired to rest. Besides, I was getting deep into the interior of Africa, and was in the neighbourhood of the Fans, the most warlike tribe that inhabited the country. So I barricaded my hut, got my ammunition ready, saw that my guns were all right, and then lay awake for a long time, before I could go to sleep.

CHAPTER VIII.

I ARRIVE AMONG THE CANNIBALS—THEIR SPEARS, BOWS, AND BATTLE-AXES—THEY TAKE ME FOR A SPIRIT—THEIR KING SHAKES WHEN HE SEES ME—I GIVE HIM A LOOKING-GLASS—IT ASTONISHES HIM.

We were, at last, near the Fan country. We had passed the last Mbichos village, and were on our way to the villages of the *man-eaters*.

I remember well the first Fan village I approached. It stood on the summit of a high hill in the mountains. All its inhabitants were very much excited when they perceived we were coming towards it, through the plantation path; for the trees around the hill had beencut down. The men were armed to the teeth, as we entered the village, and I knew not whether hundreds of spears and poisoned arrows might not be thrown at me, and I be killed on the spot. What dreadful spears those cannibals had; they were all barbed. Each man had several in his hand; and, besides, had a shield made of elephant's hide, to protect himself with. Others were armed with huge knives, and horrible-looking battle-axes, or with bows and poisoned arrows.

Wild shouts of astonishment, which, for all I knew, were war-shouts, greeted me as I entered the village. I must own that I felt not quite at my ease. How wild and fierce these men looked! They were most scantily dressed. When they shouted, they showed their teeth, which were filed to a point, and coloured black. Their open mouths put me uncomfortably in mind of a tomb; for how many human creatures each of these men had eaten!

How ugly the women looked! They were all tattooed, and nearly naked. They fled with their children into their houses, as I passed through the street, in which I saw, here and there, human bones lying about. Yes, human bones from bodies that had been devoured by them! Such are my recollections of my first entrance into a village of cannibals.

The village was strongly fenced, or palisaded; and on the poles were several skulls of human beings and of gorillas. There was but a single street, about two-thirds of a mile long. On each side of this were low huts, made of the bark of trees.

I had hardly entered the village when I perceived some bloody remains, which appeared to me to be human. Presently we passed a woman who was running as fast as she could towards her hut. She bore in her hand a piece of a human thigh, just as we should go to market and carry thence a joint or steak.

This was a very large village. At last we arrived at the palaver house. Here I was left alone with Mbéné for a little while. There was great shouting going on at a little distance, at the back of some houses. One of them said they had been busy dividing the body of a dead man, and that there was not enough for all.

They flocked in presently, and soon I was surrounded by an immense crowd. Not far from me was a ferocious-looking fellow. On one arm he supported a very large shield, made of an elephant's hide, and of the thickest part of the skin, while in his other hand he held a prodigious war-knife, which he could have slashed through a man in a jiffy.

Some in the crowd were armed with cross-bows, from which were shot either iron-headed arrows, or the little, insignificant-looking, but really most deadly darts, tipped with poison. These are made of slender, harmless reeds, a foot long, whose sharpened ends are dipped in a deadly vegetable poison, which these people know how to make. These poisoned darts are so light that they would blow away, if simply laid in the groove of the bow. Hence they use a kind of sticky gum to hold them.

The handle of the bow is ingeniously split; and, by a little peg, that acts as a trigger, the bow-string is disengaged. The bow is very stiff and strong, and sends the arrow to a great distance. As you see by the representation of a Fan bowman, they have to sit down and apply both feet to the middle of the bow, while they pull with all their strength on the string to bend it back.

These little poisoned arrows are much dreaded by them, and are very carefully kept in little bags, which are made of the skin of wild animals.

Some bore on their shoulders the terrible war-axe. A single blow of this axe suffices to split a humanskull. I saw that some of these axes, as well as their spears and other ironwork, were beautifully ornamented.

The war-knife, which hangs by their side, is a terrible weapon. It is used in hand-to-hand conflict, and is designed to be thrust through the enemy's body. There was also another sort of huge knife used by some of the men in the crowd before me. It was a foot long, about eight inches wide, and is used to cut through the shoulders of an adversary. It must do tremendous execution.

A few of the men had also a very singular pointed axe, which is thrown from a distance. When thrown, it strikes with the point down, and inflicts a terrible wound. They handle it with great dexterity. The object aimed at with this axe is the head. The point penetrates to the brain, and kills the victim immediately.

The spears were six or seven feet long, and are ingeniously adapted to inflict terrible wounds. They are thrown with an accuracy and a force which never ceased to astonish me. The long, slender staff fairly whistles through the air; and woe to the man who is within twenty or thirty yards of their reach.

Most of the knives and axes were ingeniously sheathed in covers made of snake or antelope skins, or of human skin. These sheaths were slung round the shoulder or neck by cords, which permit the weapon to hang at the side, out of the wearer's way.

These Fan warriors had no armour. Their only weapon of defence is the huge shield of elephant hide, of which I spoke to you. It is three and a half feet long, by two and a half feet wide.

Besides their weapons, many of the men wore a small knife, as a table-knife, or jack-knife.

From this description of the men by whom I was surrounded, you may judge with what amazement I looked around me, with my guns in my hands. It was a grand sight to see such a number of stalwart, martial, fierce-looking fellows, fully armed, and ready for any desperate fray, gathered together.

Finer-looking savages I never saw; and I could easily believe them to be brave; and the completeness of their war-like equipments proved that fighting is a favourite pastime with them. No wonder they are dreaded by all their neighbours!

Here was I, at this time only a lad, alone in the midst of them.

Presently came the king, a ferocious-looking fellow. His body was naked. His skin in front was painted red, and his chest, stomach, and back were tattooed in a rude but effective manner. He was covered with charms, and he wore round his neck a necklace made with leopard's teeth. He was fully armed. Most of the Fans wore queues; but the queue of Ndiayai, the king, was the biggest of all, and terminated in two tails, in which were strung brass rings. His beard was plaited in several plaits, which contained white beads. His teeth were filed sharp to a point. He looked like a perfect glutton of human flesh.

I looked around me in a cool, impassive manner. Ndiayai, the king, fairly shook at the sight of me. He had refused to come and see me, at first, from a belief that he would die in three days after setting eyes on me. But Mbéné had persuaded him to come. Ndiayai was accompanied by the queen, the ugliest woman I ever saw, and very old. She was called Mashumba. She was nearly naked, her only covering being a strip of cloth about four inches wide, made of the soft bark of a tree, and dyed red. Her body was tattooed in the most fanciful manner; her skin, from long exposure, had become rough and knotty. She wore two enormous iron anklets, and had, in her ears, a pair ofcopper rings, two inches in diameter. I could easily put my little fingers in the holes through which the earrings passed.

The people looked at me, wondered at my hair, but never ceased to look at my feet. "Look at the strange being," said they to each other, "his feet are not of the colour of his face, and he has no toes!"

Finally, the king said to Mbéné that, when surrounded by his people, he was not afraid of anybody.

I could well believe him. When fighting they must look perfect devils.

When night came I entered my house, and looked about to see how I could barricade myself for the night; for I did not fancy putting myself entirely at the mercy of these savage Fans. Their weapons had been sufficient to show me that they were men who were not afraid to fight. I told Mbéné to send for Ndiayai. The king came, and I presented him a large bunch of white beads, a looking-glass, a file, fire-steels, and some gun-flints. His countenance beamed with joy. I never saw such astonishment as he exhibited when I held the looking-glass before his face. At first he did not know what to make of it, and did not want to take the glass, till Mbéné told him that he had one. He put his tongue out, and he saw it reflected in the looking-glass. Then he shut one eye, and made faces; then he showed his hands before the looking-glass—one finger—two fingers—three fingers. He became speechless, and with all I had given him, he went away as "happy as a king"; and "every inch a (savage) king" he was.

Shortly afterwards, Mashumba, the queen, thinking that probably I had something for her, also came and brought me a basketful of plantains. They were cooked. At once the idea rushed into my mind, that perhaps the very same pot that cooked the plantainshad cooked a Fan's head in the morning; and I began to have a horrible loathing of the flesh-pots of these people. I would not have cooked in their pots for the world.

A little after dark, all became silent in the village. I barred my little bit of a door as well as I could with my chest, and, lying down on that dreadful Fan bed, I placed my gun by my side, and tried hard, but in vain, to go to sleep. I wondered how many times human flesh had entered the hut I was in. I thought of all I had seen during the day, which I have related to you. The faces of those terrible warriors, and the implements of war, were before my eyes though it was pitch dark.

Was I afraid? Certainly not. What feeling was it that excited me? I cannot tell you. It was certainly not fear; for if anyone the next day had offered to take me back where I came from, I should have declined the offer.

Probably I was agitated by the novel and horrible sights that had greeted my eyes, and which exceeded all my previous conceptions of Africa. Now and then I thought that as these men not only killed people, but ate them also, they might perhaps be curious to try how I tasted.

Hour after hour passed, and I could not get to sleep. I said my bed was a dreadfully bad one. It was a frame composed of half a dozen large round bamboos. I might as well have tried to sleep on a pile of cannonballs. Finally, I succeeded in going to sleep, holding my gun tightly under my arm.

When I got up in the morning, and went out at the back of the house, I saw a pile of ribs, leg and arm bones, and skulls, piled together. The cannibals must have had a grand fight, not long before, and devoured all their prisoners of war.

In what was I to wash my face? I resolved at last not to wash at all.

CHAPTER IX.

AN ELEPHANT HUNT.

After a few days the Fans began to get accustomed to me, and I to them; and we were the best friends in the world.

They are great hunters. One day a woman returning from the plantations brought news, that she had seen elephants; and that one of the plantain fields had been entirely destroyed by them. This was an event of common occurrence in the country; for theelephants are not very particular, and whatever they like they take; not caring a bit how much hunger they may occasion among the poor natives.

When the news arrived, a wild shout of joy spread among the villagers. The grim faces of the Fans smiled; and in doing so, showed their ugly filed teeth. "We are going to kill elephants," they all shouted. "We are going to have plenty of meat to eat," shrieked the women.

So in the evening a war-dance took place; a war-dance of cannibals! It was the wildest scene I ever saw. It was pitch-dark; and the torches threw a dim light around us, and showed the fantastic forms of these wild men. Really it was a wild scene. They were all armed as if they were going to war. How they gesticulated! What contortions they made! What a tumult they raised! How their wild shouts echoed from hill to hill, and died away in the far distance! They looked like demons. Their skins were painted of different colours; and, as the dancing went on, their bodies became warm, and shone as if they had been dipped in oil.

Suddenly a deafening shout of the whole assemblage seemed to shake the earth. Their greatest warrior (Leopard) came to dance. Leopard was, it appears, the bravest of them all. He had killed more people in war than anybody else. He had given more human food to his fellow-townsmen than many other warriors put together. Hence they all admired and praised him; and a song describing his feats of arms was sung by those who surrounded him. How ferocious he looked! He was armed to the teeth. He had a spear like one of those I have already described. A long knife hung by its side, and the hand that held the shield carried a battle-axe also. In dancing, he acted at times as if he were defending himself against an attack; at othertimes, as if he were himself attacking somebody. Once or twice I really thought he meant to throw his spear at someone. I could hardly breathe while looking at him. He appeared actually to be a demon. Finally he stopped from sheer exhaustion, and others took his place.

The next day the men furbished up their arms. I myself cleaned my guns, and got ready for the chase; so that, if I could get a chance, I might send a bullet through an elephant.

The war-dish was cooked. It is a mixture of herbs, and is supposed to inspire people with courage. They rubbed their bodies with it, and then we started. There were about five hundred men. After leaving the village we divided into several parties. Each party was well acquainted with the forest, and knew just where to go. The march was conducted in perfect silence, so that we might not alarm the elephants. After proceeding six hours we arrived not far from the hunting-ground where the elephants were supposed to be. The Fans built shelters, and these were hardly finished when it began to rain very hard.

The next day some Fans went out to explore the woods, and I joined the party. The fallen trees, the broken-down limbs, the heavy footprints, and the trampled underbrush, showed plainly that there had been many elephants about. There were no regular walks, and they had strayed at random in the forest.

When the elephants are pleased with a certain neighbourhood, they remain there a few days. When they have eaten all the food they like, and nothing remains, they go on to some other place.

The forest here, as everywhere else, was full of rough, strong, climbing plants, many of which reach to the top of the tallest trees. They are of every size; some bigger than a man's thigh, while many are aslarge as the ropes of which the rigging of a ship is made. These creepers the natives twist together; and, after working very hard, they succeed in constructing a huge fence, or obstruction. Of course, it is not sufficient to hold the elephant; but when he gets entangled in its meshes, it is strong enough to check him in his flight, till the hunters can have time to kill him. When an elephant is once caught, they surround the huge beast, and put an end to his struggles by incessant discharges of their spears and guns.

While the others worked, I explored the forest. Seeing that the men were careful in avoiding a certain place, I looked down on the ground, and saw nothing. Then, looking up, I saw an immense piece of wood suspended by the wild creepers, high in the air; and, fixed in it at intervals, I saw several large, heavy, sharp pointed pieces of iron pointing downwards. The rope that holds up this contrivance is so arranged that the elephant cannot help touching it, if he passes underneath. Then the *hanou* (such is the name given to the trap) is loosened, it falls with a tremendous force on his back; the iron points pierce his body, and the piece of wood, in falling, generally breaks his spine.

I also saw in different places, large, deep ditches, intended as pitfalls for the elephant. When he runs away, or roams around at night, he often falls into these pits, and that is the end of him; for, in falling, he generally breaks his legs. Sometimes, when the natives go and visit the pit they have made, they find nothing but the bones of the elephant and his ivory tusks.

The fence that the natives had made must have been several miles long, and in many places was several rows deep; and now there were elephant pits beside, and the *hanous*.

We were, you must remember, in a mountainous country; and I could scarcely believe my eyes when I saw plainly the footprints of this animal where I myself had to hold to the creepers to be able to ascend.

When everything was ready, part of the men went silently and hid themselves upon the limbs or besides the trunks of trees near the barrier or "tangle." Others of us took a circuitous route in an opposite direction from that in which we had come. After we had got miles away from the "tangle," we formed a chain as long in extent as the fence, and moved forward, forming a semi-circle, with the men ten or twenty yards apart from each other.

Presently, all along the line the hunting horns were sounded, wild shouts were sent up, and, making all the noise they could, the Fans advanced in the direction of the "tangle." The elephants were entrapped. Hearing the noise, of course they moved away from us, breaking down everything before them in their flight. If they tried to go to the right, they heard the same wild shouts; if they tried to go to the left, they heard the same. There was no other way for them to go but straight ahead; and there, though they did not know it, were the tangle, the pits, and the *hanous*. They were going to surer death than if they had tried to break our lines; for then most, if not all of them, would have escaped. We were too far from each other to hinder them.

Onward we pressed, the circle of those giving chase becoming smaller and smaller, and the crashing of the underbrush more distinct, as we approached the elephants in their flight. The men's countenances became excited. They got their spears in readiness; and soon we came in sight of the tangles. What an extraordinary sight lay before me; I could distinguishone elephant, enraged, terrified, tearing at everything with his trunk and feet, but all in vain! The tough creepers of the barrier in no instance gave way before him. Spear after spear was thrown at him. The Fans were everywhere, especially up on the trees, where they were out of the reach of the elephant. The huge animal began to look like a gigantic porcupine, he was stuck so full of spears. Poor infuriated beast! I thought he was crazy. Every spear that wounded him made him more furious! But his struggles were in vain. He had just dropped down when I came close to him; and to end his sufferings, I shot him through the ear. After a few convulsions of limb all became quiet. He was dead.

Some of the elephants had succeeded in going through the tangle, and were beyond reach.

Four elephants had been slain; and I was told that a man had been killed by one of the elephants, which turned round and charged his assailants. This man did not move off in time, and was trampled under foot by the monstrous beast. Fortunately, the elephant got entangled; and, in an instant, he was covered with spears, and terribly wounded. After much loss of blood he dropped down lifeless.

I am sure you will agree with me, after the description I have given of a Fan elephant hunt, that the men of this tribe are gifted with remarkable courage and presence of mind.

They have certain rules for hunting the elephant. These tell you never to approach an elephant, except from behind; he cannot turn very fast, and you have, therefore, time to make your escape. He generally rushes blindly forward. Great care must also be taken that the strong creepers, which are so fatal to the elephant, do not also catch and entangle the hunters themselves. A man lying in wait to spear an elephantshould always choose a stout tree, in order that the infuriated beast, should he charge at it, may not uproot it.

The next day, there was a dance round the elephant, while the fetich-man cut a piece from one of the hind legs. This was intended for their idol. The meat was cooked in presence of the fetich-man, and of those who had speared the elephant. As soon as all the meat had been cooked they danced round it; and a piece was sent into the woods for the spirit to feed upon, if he liked. The next day, the meat was all cut up in small pieces, then hung up and smoked.

The cooking and smoking lasted three days, and I can assure you it is the toughest meat I ever tasted. Of course, like the Fans, I had no other food; and for three days I ate nothing but elephant meat. I wish I could give you a notion how it tastes; but really I do not know what to compare it with. Beef, mutton, lamb, pork, venison, make not the slightest approach to a resemblance: and as for poultry, such a comparison would be positively aggravating!

The proboscis being one of the favourite morsels, a large piece of it was given to me. The foot is another part reputed to be a great dainty, and two feet were sent me, together with a large piece of the leg for a roast.

But the meat was so tough that I had to boil it for twelve hours; and then I believe it was as tough as ever; it seemed to be full of gristle. So, the next day, I boiled it again for twelve hours; all my trouble, however, was unavailing, for it was still hopelessly tough! I may say, that the more I ate of elephant meat the more I got to dislike it. I do not think I shall ever hanker after elephant steak as long as I live. I wonder if you boys would like it? I wish I had some, and could induce you to taste of it. I aminclined to think you would agree with me, and never desire to renew your acquaintance with it.

How glad I was when I returned to Ndiayai village; and no wonder, for we had rain every day in the woods. As for the poor man who had been killed by the elephant, his body was sent to another clan to be devoured; for the cannibals do not eat their own people.

CHAPTER X.

LIFE AMONG THE CANNIBALS—CURIOUS MUSICAL
INSTRUMENTS—COOKING UTENSILS—A BLACKSMITH'S
BELLOWS AND ANVIL—CANNIBAL DIET.

After we reached Ndiayai, I went back to my little hut, and found
everything I had left there. I had hidden my powder and shot in different
places, and had dug holes in which to hide my beads.

The news had spread among the surrounding cannibal villages that the
spirit, as they called me, wasstill in the village of Ndiayai, and the people
flocked to see me. Among those who came to see me, was a chief of the
name of Oloko. He gave me the long war knife, of which you have seen a
drawing, and explained to me how it had several times gone right through a
man.

Mbéné went away for a while, and left me entirely alone with these
cannibals. During his absence I studied the habits of these strange people;
and you may be sure that wherever I went I kept my eyes wide open.

By the way, I see I have omitted to give a description of the town of King
Ndiayai. It was a very large town, composed of a single street. When I say a
large town, I do not mean, of course, that it could bear any comparison as
to size with London, Paris, or New York. I mean that it was a large town
for this part of Africa. It contained five or six hundred men. The houses
were quite small, and were all made of the bark of trees; none of them had
windows. They were nearly all of the same size.

Strange to say, these Fans seemed to be very fond of music, and very funny
instruments they make use of. To hear some of their music would make
you laugh. They have not the slightest idea of what we consider harmony in
sound; but they evidently have a great liking for music after their own
notion. It is very much the same with their dancing. They have not the
slightest idea of the dances in use with us, such as waltzes, galops, polkas,
or quadrilles; and I am sure if they were to see us dancing in our fashion,
they would laugh quite as much as you would laugh if you could see them
capering in their uncouth style.

Like all the savage tribes of Africans, they are very fond of the tom-tom, or
drum. Those drums are of different sizes, but many are from four to six
feet inlength, and about ten inches in diameter at one end, but only six or
seven at the other. The wood is hollowed out quite thin, and skins of
animals are stretched tightly over the ends. The drummer holds the tom-
tom slantingly between his legs; and, with two sticks, he beats furiously
upon the larger end of the drum, which is held uppermost. Sometimes they

beat upon it with their hands. The people form a circle round the tom-tom, and dance and sing, keeping time with it. They often invited me to hear them.

But now I am going to speak to you of a far more curious instrument. It is called by these cannibals the handja; and I never saw it except among their tribes.

Ndiayai was very fond of hearing the handja, and I often went to his shed to hear someone play upon it. Sometimes, on these occasions, Ndiayai would come out surrounded by Queen Mashumba and some of his other wives, and listen for an hour or two to the music of the handja.

I give you a representation of the handja (*see* p. 78), so you will understand better when I describe it to you.

It consists of a light reed frame, about three feet long, and eighteen inches wide, in which are set, and securely fastened, a number of hollow gourds. The handja I saw contained seven gourds. These gourds are covered by strips of a hard, red wood, found in the forest. These gourds and cylinders, as you see, are of different sizes, so graduated that they form a regular series of notes. Each gourd has a little hole which is covered with a skin thinner than parchment. And what kind of skin do you think it was? It was the skin of the very large spider which abounds in that country, and from which I should not care to receive a bite, it is so poisonous.

The performer sits down, with the frame across his knees, and strikes the strips lightly with a stick. There are two sticks, one of hard wood, the other of much softer wood. The instrument is played on the same principle as a chime of bells, or an instrument used in France, and which, perhaps, some of you have seen, composed of a series of glasses. The tone of the handja is very clear and good, and though their tunes were rude, they played them with considerable skill.

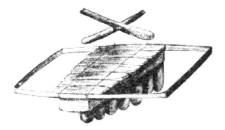

THE HANDJA.

The Fans work iron better than any tribe I met with. They are very good blacksmiths. Their warlike habits have made iron a very necessary article to them. It is very plentiful in their mountainous country.

Before you is a picture of two Fan blacksmiths. Look at the curious bellows they have. It is made of two short, hollow cylinders of wood, surmounted by skins, very well fitted on, and having an appropriate valve for letting in the air. As you see, the bellows-blower is on his knees, moving down these coverings with great rapidity. There are two small woodenpipes, connected with two iron tubes which go into the fire.

The anvil, as you see in the picture, is a solid piece of iron. The sharp end is stuck into the ground; and the blacksmith sits alongside his anvil, and beats his iron with a singular-looking hammer, clumsy in form, and with no handle; in fact it is merely made of a heavy piece of iron.

The blacksmiths sometimes spend many days in making a battle-axe, knife or spear. They make, also, their own cooking utensils and water-jugs. These are of the shape you see in the picture before you. They also make their own pipes, for they are great smokers. Some of their pipes are not at all ungraceful in shape.

Besides the water-jug, they frequently use the calabash, as a vessel to carry water in; and some of their calabashes are really pretty, and very nicely ornamented. Some of the spoons, with which they eat their human broth, are very beautiful. They are made of various woods, and sometimes of ivory.

It is quite sickening to think what horrible people these Fans are! Such inveterate cannibals are they, that they even eat the poor wretches who die of disease. As I was talking to the king one day, some Fans brought in a dead body, which they had bought or bartered for, in a neighbouring town, and which was to be divided among them. I could see that the man had died of some disease; for the body was very lean. They came round it with their knives; and Ndiayai left me to superintend the distribution. I could not stand this; and when I saw them getting ready, I left the spot, and went to my hut. Afterwards, I could hear them growing noisy over the division of their horrid spoil.

In fact, the Fans seem to be perfect ghouls. Those who live far in the interior practise unblushingly theirhorrid custom of eating human flesh. It appears they do not eat the dead of their own family, but sell the corpse to some other clan, or make an agreement that when one of their number dies they will return the body in exchange.

Until I saw these things I could not believe a story I had often heard related among the Mpongwe tribe, which is as follows: A party of Fans once came down to the seashore to view the ocean. While there, they actually stole a freshly-buried body from the cemetery, and cooked and ate it. Another body was taken by them and conveyed into the woods, where they cut it up, and smoked the flesh. These acts created a great excitement among the Mpongwes.

But you must not think that the Fans are continually eating human flesh. They eat it when they can get it, but not every day. They kill no one on purpose to be eaten.

One day Ndiayai took me to an Osheba town, the king of which tribe was his friend; and let me tell you that the Oshebas were also great man-eaters, like the Fans, whom they greatly resemble in appearance. The chief of that Osheba village was called Bienbakay.

The Fans are the handsomest and most resolute-looking set of negroes I have ever seen in the interior. Eating human flesh does not seem to disagree with them, though I have since seen other Fan tribes whose men had not the fine appearance of these mountaineers. Here, as everywhere else, the character of the country doubtless has much to do with the matter of bodily health and growth. These cannibals were living among the mountains, and had come from still higher mountain regions, and this accounts for their being so robust and hardy.

The strangest thing in connection with the Fans, next to their hideous cannibalism, is their constantencroachments upon the land westward. Year by year they have been advancing nearer to the sea. Town after town has been settled by them on the banks of the Gaboon river. In fact, they seem to be a conquering race, driving every other tribe before them.

The colour of these people is dark brown rather than black. They feed much upon manioc and the plantain. They have also two or three kinds of yams, splendid sugar-cane, and squashes, all of which they cultivate with considerable success. Manioc seemed to be the favourite food. Enormous quantities of squashes are raised, chiefly for the seeds, which, when pounded and prepared in their fashion, are much prized by them, and I confess I relished this food myself. At a certain season, when the squash is ripe, their villages seem covered with the seeds, which everybody spreads out to dry. When dried they are packed in leaves, and placed over the fireplaces in the smoke, to keep off an insect which also feeds upon them. They are all suspended by a cord, for, besides being infested by insects, they are subject to the depredations of mice and rats, both of which are fond of them.

The process of preparation is very tedious. A portion of the seeds is boiled, and each seed is divested of its skin; then the mass of pulp is put into a rude wooden mortar and pounded, a vegetable oil being mixed with it before it is cooked.

While on the subject of the food of the cannibals, I ought to mention that they do not sell the bodies of their chiefs, kings, or great men; these receive burial, and remain undisturbed. It is probable also that they do not eat the corpses of people who die of special diseases.

CHAPTER XI.

JOURNEY TO YOONGOOLAPAY—HUNTING WITH NETS—THE TERRIBLE BASHIKONAY ANTS.

On my way to the seashore from the cannibal country, I had a good deal of trouble. I had taken quite another route to come back; Mbéné and his people left me on the banks of a river called the Noya, at the village of a chief called Wanga. From there I pushed my way towards Yoongoolapay, a village, whose chief is called Alapay. But before reaching that place, we came one evening to avillage called Ezongo. The inhabitants, seeing our heavy loads, turned out with the greatest amount of enthusiasm to receive me. Their ardour cooled somewhat when they learned the contents of my packages, for they were the birds and animals I had collected. The rascally chief, thinking I must place a great value on things I had gone so far to get, determined to detain me till I paid a heavy price to get away; and for a while things looked as if I should have a good deal of trouble. The king, urged on by his people, who seemed to be a greedy set of rascals, insisted on his price, which would have left me empty-handed.

At last my Mbicho guides from the Noya tried to settle the matter. They were wise enough to get the king to come to me with them alone. I gave the rascal a coat and an old shirt, and I told him, what was literally true, that I was very poor, and could not pay what his people wanted. After this palaver he went out at once and harangued the turbulent extortioners.

So I passed on safely to the village of my old friend, King Alapay, whom I had known before, and who was very glad to see me again. He asked me to stay some days; and being really worn out with constant exposure, much anxiety, and frequent annoyance, I determined to do so. His village is charmingly situated upon a high hill, which overlooks the surrounding country, and has a beautiful stream skirting its base. Moreover, I found the people very kind, peaceable, and hospitable.

A considerable number of independent Mbicho villages lay within a circuit of a few miles, the inhabitants of which lived in great harmony with one another, having prudently intermarried to such a degree that they really constitute a large family. I was made welcome among them all, and spent some very pleasant days in hunting with these kind-hearted people, andparticularly in that kind of sport called by them *asheza*, or net-hunting, a practice very common among the bakalai, who called it *ashinga*.

This singular sport is very much practised in this part of Africa; and, as it is generally successful, it is a local amusement, and brings out the best traits of the natives. I was always very fond of it.

The ashinga nets are generally made of the fibres of the bark of a kind of tree, which are twisted into stout cords. They are from sixty to eighty feet long, and four to five feet high; and every well-to-do village owns at least one. But, as few villages have enough nets to make a great spread, it generally happens that several unite in a grand hunt, and divide the proceeds, the game caught in any particular net falling to the share of its owners.

The first day we went out, the people of half a dozen villages met together at an appointed place, the men of each bringing their nets. Then we set out for a spot about ten miles off, where they had a clearing in the dense woods, which had been used before, and was one of their hunting-grounds. We moved along in silence, so as not to alarm the animals which might be near our ground. The dogs—for dogs are used in this hunt—were kept still, and close together.

Finally, we arrived on the ground, and the work of spreading the toils began. Each party stretched a single net, tying it up by creepers to the lower branches of trees. As all worked in the same direction, and each took care to join his net to that of his neighbour, in a very short time we had a line of netting running in a wide half circle, and at least half a mile long.

This done, a party went out on each side, to guard against the chance of escape, and the rest of us were ready to beat the bush. We started at about a mile from the nets, and, standing about fifty yards from each other, we advanced gradually, shouting and making all the noise we could, at the same time keeping our arms in readiness to shoot or spear down anything which might come in our way.

Though this very spot had been frequently used for net-hunting, and was therefore better cleared than the neighbouring woods, yet we were obliged to proceed almost step by step. Nearly every native carried, besides his gun, a heavy cutlass or bill, with which it was necessary literally to hew out a way, the vines and creepers making a network which only the beasts of the forest could glide through without trouble.

As we advanced, so did the men that guarded the flanks; and thus our party gradually closed round the prey. Presently we began to hear shouts, but we could see nothing; and I could only hold my gun in readiness and pray that my neighbours might not shoot me by mistake; for they are fearfully reckless when on a chase.

The dogs had for some time been let loose. At last we came in sight of the nets. We had caught a gazelle of very minute size, called *ncheri*. It is a very graceful little animal, and would make a pretty pet, though I have never seen one tamed. A large antelope also was brought to bay, and shot before

I came up; and another antelope, being shot at and missed, rushed forward and got entangled in the net.

Having drawn this cover, we gathered up the nets and went off with the dogs, who enjoyed the sport vastly, to try another place. After walking about three-quarters of an hour we again spread our nets. Here we had better luck, catching a considerable number of antelopes, gazelles, and some smaller animals. It was pretty busy work for us. Nearly allthe animals got very much entangled, and the more they tried to get through the nets the more they became bewildered.

Before breaking up, all the game caught was laid together, that all might see it. And now I had an opportunity to notice the curious little sharp-eared dogs, about a foot high, which had been so useful in driving the animals into our toils. They stood looking at their prizes with eager and hungry eyes. These dogs often go and hunt for themselves; and it is no unusual thing for half-a-dozen dogs to drive an antelope to the neighbourhood of their village, when their barking arouses the hunters, who come out and kill their quarry.

It was almost dark when we returned to the village of Alapay. One antelope was put aside for me, being a peculiar species which I wanted to stuff; and the rest of the meat was immediately divided. The villagers were delighted at our luck. We were all very hungry, and cooking began at once. I could hardly wait for the dinner, which was one worthy of an emperor's palate. It consisted of plantain, cooked in various ways, and venison of the tenderest sort, stewed in lemon-juice, and afterwards roasted on charcoal.

I was glad to go to bed early, for I felt very tired. I had travelled during the day very nearly thirty miles.

But I had scarcely got sound asleep when I was fairly turned out of the house by a furious attack of the Bashikonay ants. They were already upon me when I jumped up, and I was bitten by them terribly. I ran out into the street, and called for help and torches. The natives came out, the lights were struck, and presently I was relieved. But now we found that the whole village was attacked. A great army of ants was pouring in on us, attracted doubtless by the meat in the houses, which they had smelt afar off. My unfortunate antelope had probably brought them to my door. All hands had to turn out to defend themselves. We built little cordons of fires, which kept them away from places they had not entered, and in this way protected our persons from their attacks. We scattered hot ashes and boiling water right and left; and towards morning, having eaten everything they could get at, they left us in peace. As was to be expected, my antelope was literally eaten up—not a morsel left.

The vast number, the sudden appearance, and the ferocity of these frightful creatures never ceased to astonish me. On this occasion they had come actually in millions. The antelope on which they fed was a vast mass of living ants, which we could not approach; and it was only when many fires were lighted that they were forced from their onward and victorious course, which they generally pursue. Then, however, they retreated in parties with the greatest regularity, vast numbers remaining to complete the work of destruction. Little would I give for the life of a man who should be tied up to a tree when these ants pass that way and attack him; in two or three hours nothing would be left of him but the bare bones.

CHAPTER XII.

RETURNING TO THE COAST—CAVERNS AND WATERFALLS IN THE HIGHLANDS—CROSSING A RIVER ON MANGROVE ROOTS—STIRRING UP A BIG SNAKE—A MUTUAL SCARE.

I left the good villagers of Yoongoolapay, and pursued my way to the seashore. On the route we came to a high ridge, or plateau. This was the highest land I had seen between the Moonda and the Mani, and it is probable that, if it had not been for the trees, I should have seen the ocean very well. Along this ridge were strewn some of the most extraordinary boulders I ever saw. These immense blocks of granite covered the ground in every direction. Several of them were between twenty and thirty feet high, and about fifty feet long.

Near the largest of these granite masses a huge rock rose some forty or fifty feet out of the ground. I saw an opening in the solid rock, leading to a fine large cavern. It had no doubt been made by the hands of man; it was not of natural formation, for the entrance had evidently been cut out of the solid rock by human beings; and now it was much used by the natives as a house to stop in over night when they were travelling to and fro. Its vast opening admits such a flood of sunlight and air that it is not likely to be used as a lair for wild beasts. We saw the remains of several fires inside, but I am bound to say we saw also the tracks of leopards and other dangerous beasts on the outside, for which reason I did not care to sleep there.

While exploring the cavern I thought several times I heard a trickling, which was almost like the noise of rain, and which I had not noticed before, probably on account of the great shouting of my men. But when we got out I was surprised to find not a cloud in the sky. Turning for an explanation to Alapay, he led me along a path, and as we went forward the trickling noise gradually grew into the sound of rushing waters. Presently we came to the edge of a steep declivity, and here I saw before and around me a most charming landscape, the centre of which was a most beautiful waterfall. A little stream, which meandered along the slope of the plateau, and which had hitherto escaped our view, had here worn its way through a vast granite block which barred its course. Rushing through the narrow and almost circular hole in this block, it fell in one silvery leap perpendicularly forty or fifty feet. The lower level of the stream ran along between high, steep banks covered with trees, the right bank being quite abrupt. It was a miniature Niagara. Clear, sparkling, and pure as it could be, the water rushed down to its pebbly bed—a sight so charming that I sat down for some time and feasted my eyes upon it.

I then determined to have a view from below. After some difficult climbing we got to the bottom, and there beheld, under the fall, a large hole in the perpendicular face of the rock, which evidently formed the mouth of a cavern. The opening of the cavern was partly hidden by the waterfall, and was cut through solid rock. Between the opening and the waterfall there were a few feet of clear space, so that by going sideways one could make good his entrance into the cavern without receiving a shower bath.

I determined to enter this cavern; but before venturing I went first and tried to get a peep at the inside. It was so dark that I could see nothing, so it was not very inviting. We lit torches; I took my revolver and gun, and, accompanied by two men, who also were armed with guns, we entered. How dark it was! Once inside, we excited the astonishment of a vast number of huge vampire bats. There were thousands and thousands of them. They came and fluttered around our lights, threatening each moment to leave us in darkness, and the motion of their wings filled the cavern with a dull thunderous or booming roar. It really looked an awful place, and the dim light of our torches gave to every shadow a fantastic form.

The cavern was rather rough inside. When we had advanced about one hundred yards we came to a stream, or puddle of water, extending entirely across the floor, and barring our way. My men, who had gone thus far under protest, now desired to return, and urged me notto go into the water. It might be very deep; it might be full of horrible water snakes; all sorts of wild beasts might be beyond, and land snakes also. At the word snake I hesitated, for I confess to a great dread of serpents in the dark, or in a confined place, where a snake is likely to get the advantage of a man. A cold shudder ran through me at the thought that, once in the water, many snakes might come and swim round me, and perhaps twist themselves about me as they do around the branches of trees. So I paused and reflected.

While peering into the darkness beyond I thought I saw two eyes, like bright sparks or coals of fire, gleaming savagely at us. Could it be a leopard, or what? Without thinking of the consequences, I levelled my gun at the shining objects and fired. The report, for a moment, deafened us. Then came a redoubled rush of the great hideous bats. It seemed to me that millions of these animals suddenly launched out upon us from all parts of the surrounding gloom. Some of these got caught in my clothes. Our torches were extinguished in an instant, and, panic-stricken, we all made for the cavern's mouth. I had visions of enraged snakes springing after and trying to catch me. We were all glad to reach daylight once more, and nothing could have induced us to try the darkness again. I confess that, though I think it takes a good deal to frighten me, I did not at all relish remaining there in entire darkness.

The scene outside was as charming as that within was hideous. I stood a long time looking at one of the most beautiful landscapes I ever beheld in Africa. It was certainly not grand, but extremely pretty. Before me, the little stream whose fall over the cliff filled the forest with a gentle murmur, resembling very much, as I have said, when far enough off, the patteringof a shower of rain, ran along between steep banks, the trees of which seemed to meet above it. Away down the valley we could see its course, traced like a silver line over the plain, till it was lost to our sight in a denser part of the forest.

I have often thought of these caverns since I saw them, and I have regretted that I did not pay more attention to them. If I had made my camp in the vicinity, and explored them and dug in them for days, I think that I should have been amply rewarded for the trouble. At that time I did not feel greatly interested in the subject. I had not read the works of M. Boucher de Perthes and others, or heard that the bones of animals now extinct had been discovered in caverns in several parts of Europe, and that implements made of flint, such as axes, sharp-pointed arrows, etc., etc., had been found in such places. If I had excavated I might perhaps have found the remains of charcoal fires, or other things, to prove that these caverns had been made by men who lived in Africa long before the negro. I feel certain these caverns must have been human habitations. I do not see how they could have been made except by the hand of man.

On my last journey I thought once or twice of going to them from the Fernand-Vaz, to explore and dig in them. I thought I might be rewarded for labour by discovering the bones of unknown beasts, or of some remains of primitive men.

These caverns are fortunately not far away from the sea—I should think not more than ten or fifteen miles—and are situated between the Muni and the Moonda rivers. Anyone desiring to explore them would easily find the way to them. The cavern under the waterfall would be extremely interesting to explore.

The valley itself was a pleasant wooded plain, which,it seemed, the hand of man had not yet disturbed, and whence the song of birds, the chatter of monkeys, and the hum of insects came up to us, now and then, in a confusion of sounds very pleasant to the ear.

But I could not loiter long over this scene, being anxious to reach the seashore. After we set off again we found ourselves continually crossing or following elephant tracks, so we walked very cautiously, expecting every moment to find ourselves face to face with a herd.

By-and-by the country became quite flat, the elephant tracks ceased, and presently, as we neared a stream, we came to a mangrove swamp. It was almost like seeing an old friend, or, I may say, an old enemy, for the remembrances of mosquitoes, tedious navigation, and malaria which the mangrove tree brought to my mind were by no means pleasant. It is not very pleasant to be laid up with African fever, I assure you.

From a mangrove tree to a mangrove swamp and forest is but a step. They never stand alone. Presently we stood once more on the banks of the little stream, whose clear, pellucid water, had so charmed me a little farther up the country. Now it was only a swamp, a mangrove swamp. Its bed, no longer narrow, was spread over a flat of a mile, and the now muddy water meandered slowly through an immense growth of mangroves, whose roots extended entirely across, and met in the middle, where they rose out of the mire and water like the folds of some vast serpent.

It was high tide. There was not a canoe to be had. To sleep on this side, among the mangroves, was to be eaten up by the mosquitoes, which bite much harder than those of America, for they can pierce through your trousers and drawers. This was not a very pleasant anticipation, but there seemed to be no alternative, and I had already made up my mind that I should notbe able to go to sleep. But my men were not troubled at all with unpleasant anticipations. We were to cross over, quite easily too, they said, on the roots which projected above the water, and which lay from two to three feet apart, at irregular distances.

It seemed a desperate venture, but they set out jumping like monkeys from place to place, and I followed, expecting every moment to fall in between the roots in the mud, there to be attacked, perhaps, by some noxious reptile whose rest my fall would disturb. I had to take off my shoes, whose thick soles made me more likely to slip. I gave all my baggage, and guns, and pistols to the men, and then commenced a journey, the like of which I hope never to take again. We were an hour in getting across—an hour of continual jumps and hops, and holding on. In the midst of it all a man behind me flopped into the mud, calling out, "Omemba!" in a frightful voice.

Now, *omemba* means snake. The poor fellow had put his hands on an enormous black snake, and, feeling its cold, slimy scales, he let go his hold and fell. All hands immediately began to run faster than before, both on the right and the left. There was a general panic, and every one began to shout and make all kinds of noises to frighten the serpent. The poor animal also got badly scared, and began to crawl away among the branches as fast as he could. Unfortunately his fright led him directly towards me, and a general panic ensued. Everybody ran as fast as he could to get out of danger.

Another man fell into the mud below, and added his cries to the general tumult. Two or three times I was on the point of getting a mud bath myself, but I luckily escaped. My feet were badly cut and bruised, but at last we were safe across, and I breathed freely once more, as soon after I saw the deep blue sea.

CHAPTER XIII.

CAPE LOPEZ AND AN OPEN PRAIRIE ONCE MORE—KING
BANGO AND HIS THREE HUNDRED WIVES—HIS FIVE
IDOLS—SLAVE BARRACOONS—THE CORPSE AND THE
VULTURES.

Cape Lopez is a long sandy arm of land reaching out into the sea. As you approach it from the ocean it has the appearance of overflowed land. It is so low that the bushes and the trees growing on it seem, from a distance seaward, to be set in the water.

The bay formed by Cape Lopez is about fourteen miles long. Among several small streams which empty their water into it is the Nazareth river, one of whose branches is the Fetich river. The bay has numerous shallows and small islands, and abounds in all sorts of delicious fish. On the cape itself many large turtles from the ocean come to lay their eggs. I will tell you by-and-by what a nice time I had fishing at Cape Lopez; but I have many other things to talk about before I come to that.

I arrived at Cape Lopez one evening when it was almost dark. The next morning I prepared myself for a visit to King Bango, the king of the country. The royal palace is set up on a tolerably high hill, and fronts the seashore. Between the foot of this hill and the sea there is a beautiful prairie, over which are scattered the numerous little villages called Sangatanga. I never tired of looking at this prairie. I had lived so long in the gloomy forest that it gave me great delight to see once more the green and sunlit verdure of an open meadow. I found the royal palace surrounded by a little village of huts. As I entered the village I was met by the *mafouga*, or officer of the king, who conducted me to the palace. It was an ugly-looking house of two stories, resting on pillars. The lower story consisted of a dark hall, flanked on each side by rows of small dark rooms, which looked like little cells. At the end of the hall was a staircase, steep and dirty, up which the mafouga piloted me. When I had ascended the stairs I found myself in a large room, at one end of which was seated the great King Bango, who claims to be the greatest chief of this part of Africa. He was surrounded by about one hundred of his wives.

King Bango was fat, and seemed not over clean. He wore a shirt and an old pair of pantaloons. On his head was a crown, which had been presented to him by some of his friends, the Portuguese slavers. Over his shoulders he wore a flaming yellow coat, with gilt embroidery, the cast-off garment of some rich man's lacquey in Portugal or Brazil. When I speak of a crown you must not think it was a wonderful thing, made of gold and mounted with diamonds. It was shaped like those commonly worn by actors on the stage, and was probably worth, when new, about ten dollars. Hismajesty had put round it a circlet of pure gold, made with the doubloons he got in exchange for slaves. He sat on a sofa, for he was paralyzed; and in his hand he held a cane, which also answered the purpose of a sceptre.

This King Bango, whom I have described so minutely, was the greatest slave king of that part of the coast. At that time there were large slave depôts on his territory. He is a perfect despot, and is much feared by his people. He is also very superstitious.

Though very proud, he received me kindly, for I had come recommended by his great friend, Rompochombo, a king of the Mpongwe tribe. He asked me how I liked his wives. I said, very well. He then said there were a hundred present, and that he had twice as many more, three hundred in all. Fancy three hundred wives! He also claimed to have more than six hundred children. I wonder if all these brothers and sisters could know and recognise each other!

The next night a great ball was given in my honour by the king. The room where I had been received was the ball-room. I arrived there shortly after dark, and I found about one hundred and fifty of the king's wives, and I was told that the best dancers of the country were there.

I wish you could have seen the room. It was ugly enough; there were several torches to light it; but, notwithstanding these, the room was by no means brilliantly illuminated. The king wanted only his wives to dance before me. During the whole of the evening not a single man took part in the performance; but two of his daughters were ordered to dance, and he wanted me to marry one of them.

Not far from the royal palace were three curious and very small houses, wherein were deposited five idols, which were reputed to have far greater power andknowledge than the idols or gods of the surrounding countries. They were thought to be the great protectors of the Oroungou tribe, and particularly of Sangatanga and of the king. So I got a peep inside the first house. There I saw the idol called Pangeo; he was made of wood, and looked very ugly; by his side was his wife Aleka, another wooden idol. Pangeo takes care of the king, and of his people, and watches over them at night.

I peeped also into the second little house. There I saw a large idol, called Makambi, shaped like a man, and by his side stood a female figure, Abiala his wife. Poor Makambi is a powerless god, his wife having usurped the power. She holds a pistol in her hand, with which, it is supposed, she can kill anyone she pleases; hence the natives are much afraid of her; and she receives from them a constant supply of food, and many presents (I wonder who takes the presents away). When they fall sick, they dance around her, and implore her to make them well; for these poor heathen never pray to the true God. They put their trust in wooden images, the work of their own hands.

I looked into the third house, and there I saw an idol called Numba. He had no wife with him, being a bachelor deity. He is the Oroungou Neptune and Mercury in one—Neptune in ruling the waves, and Mercury in keeping off the evils which threaten from beyond the sea.

As I came away after seeing the king, I shot at a bird sitting upon a tree, but missed it, for I had been taking quinine and was nervous. But the negroes standing around at once proclaimed that this was a "fetich bird,"—a sacred bird—and therefore I could not shoot it, even if I fired at it a hundred times.

I fired again, but with no better success. Hereupon they grew triumphant in their declarations; while I, loth to let the devil have so good a witness, loaded again, took careful aim, and, to my own satisfaction and their utter dismay, brought my bird down.

During my stay in the village, as I was one day out shooting birds in a grove, not far from my house, I saw a procession of slaves coming from one of the barracoons toward the farther end of my grove. As they came nearer, I saw that two gangs of six slaves each, all chained about the neck, were carrying a burden between them, which I knew presently to be the corpse of another slave. They bore it to the edge of the grove, about three hundred yards from my house; and, throwing it down there on the bare ground, they returned to their prison, accompanied by the overseer, who, with his whip, had marched behind them.

"Here, then, is the burying-ground of the barracoons," I said to myself sadly, thinking, I confess, of the poor fellow who had been dragged away from his home and friends; who, perhaps, had been sold by his father or relatives to die here and be thrown out as food for the vultures. Even as I stood wrapped in thought, these carrion birds were assembling, and began to darken the air above my head; ere long they were heard fighting over the corpse.

The grove, which was, in fact, but an African Aceldama, was beautiful to view from my house; and I had often resolved to explore it, or to rest in the shade of its dark-leaved trees. It seemed a ghastly place enough now as I approached it more closely. The vultures fled when they saw me, but flew only a little way, and then perched upon the lower branches of the surrounding trees, and watched me with eyes askance, as though fearful I should rob them of their prey. As I walked towards the corpse, I felt something crack under my feet. Looking down, I saw that I was already in the midst of a field of skulls and bones. I hadinadvertently stepped upon the skeleton of some poor creature who had been lying here long enough for the birds and ants to pick his bones clean, and for the rains to bleach them. I think there must have been the relics of a thousand skeletons within sight. The place had been used for many years; and the mortality in the barracoons is sometimes frightful, in spite of the care they seem to take of their slaves. Here their bodies were thrown, and here the vultures found their daily carrion. The grass had just been burnt, and the white bones scattered everywhere, gave the ground a singular, and, when the cause was known, a frightful appearance. Penetrating farther into the bush, I found several great piles of bones. This was the place, years ago—when Cape Lopez was one of the great slave markets on the West Coast, and barracoons were more numerous than they are now—where the poor dead were thrown, one upon another, till even the mouldering bones remained in high piles, as monuments of the nefarious traffic. Such was the burial-ground of the poor slaves from the interior of Africa.

CHAPTER XIV.

SLAVE BARRACOONS—A BIG SNAKE UNDER MY BED—A SLAVE SHIP OFF THE COAST.

One day I passed by an immense enclosure, protected by a fence of palisades about twelve feet high, and sharp-pointed at the top. Passing through the gate, which was standing open, I found myself in the midst of a large collection of shanties, surrounded by shady trees, under which were lying, in various positions, a great many negroes. As I walked round, I saw that the men were fastened, six together, by a little stout chain, which passed through a collar secured about the neck of each. Here and there were buckets of water for the men to drink; and they being chained together, when one of the six wanted to drink, the others had to go with him.

Then I came to a yard full of women and children. These could roam at pleasure through their yard. No men were admitted there. These people could not all understand each other's language; and you may probably wish to know who they were. They were Africans belonging to various tribes, who had been sold, some by their parents or by their families; others by the people of their villages. Some had been sold on account of witchcraft; but there were many other excuses for the traffic. They would find suddenly that a boy or girl was "dull," and so forth, and must be sold. Many of them came from countries far distant.

Some were quite merry; others appeared to be very sad, thinking that they were bought to be eaten up. They believed that the white men beyond the seas were great cannibals, and that they were to be fattened first and then eaten. In the interior, one day, a chief ordered a slave to be killed for my dinner, and I barely succeeded in preventing the poor wretch from being put to death. I could hardly make the chief believe that I did not, in my own country, live on human flesh.

Under some of the trees were huge caldrons, in which beans and rice were cooking for the slaves; and others had dried fish to eat. In the evening they were put into large sheds for the night. One of the sheds was used as a hospital.

In the midst of all this stood the white man's house—yes, the white man's house!—and in it were white men whose only business was to buy these poor creatures from the Oroungou people!

After I had seen everything, I left the barracoon—for that is the name given to such a place as I have just described. I wandered about, and it was dark before I returned to the little bamboo house which the king had given me. I got in, and then, striking a match carefully, I lighted a torch, so that I might not go to bed in darkness. You may smile when I say bed, for my couch was far from bearing any resemblance to our beds at home, with mattresses and pillows, and sheets and blankets. Travellers in equatorial Africa are utter strangers to such luxuries.

After I had lighted the torch, I cast my eyes round to see if anything had been disturbed; for a thief, so disposed, could easily break into these houses. I noticed something glittering and shining under my akoko, or bedstead. The object was so still that I did not pay any attention to it; in fact, I could not see it well by the dim light of the torch. But when I approached the bed to arrange it, I saw that the glitter was produced by the shining scales of an enormous serpent, which lay quietly coiled up there within two feet of me. What was I to do? I had fastened my door with ropes. If the snake were to uncoil itself and move about, it might, perhaps, take a spring and wind itself about me, quietly squeeze me to death, and then swallow me as he would a gazelle. These were not comforting thoughts. I was afraid to cry out for fear of disturbing the snake, which appeared to be asleep. Besides, no one could get in, as I had barricaded the only entrance, so I went quietly and unfastened the door. When everything was ready for a safe retreat, I said to myself, "I had better try to kill it." Then, looking for my guns, I saw, to my utter horror, that they were set against the wall at the back of the bed, so that the snake was between me and them. After watching the snake intently, andthinking what to do, I resolved to get my gun; so, keeping the door in my rear open, in readiness for a speedy retreat at the first sign of life in the snake, I approached on tip-toe, and, in a twinkling of an eye, grasped the gun which was loaded heavily with large shot. How relieved I felt at that moment! I was no longer the same man. Fortunately, the snake did not move. With my gun in one hand I went again towards the reptile, and, fairly placing the muzzle of the gun against it, I fired, and then ran out of the house as fast as I could.

At the noise of the gun there was a rush of negroes from all sides to know what was the matter. They thought some one had shot a man, and run into my house to hide himself; so they all rushed into it, helter-skelter; but I need not tell you they rushed out just as fast, on finding a great snake writhing about on the floor. Some had trodden upon it and been frightened out of their wits. You have no idea how they roared and shouted; but no one appeared disposed to enter the house again, so I went in cautiously myself to see how matters stood, for I did not intend to give undisputed possession of my hut so easily to Mr. Snake. I entered and looked cautiously around. The dim light of the torch helped me a little, and there I saw the snake on the ground. Its body had been cut in two by the discharge, and both ends were now flapping about the floor. At first I thought these ends were two snakes, and I did not know what to make of it; but as soon as I perceived my mistake, I gave a heavy blow with a stick on the head of the horrible creature, and finished it. Then I saw it disgorge a duck—a whole duck—and such a long duck! It looked like an enormous long-feathered sausage. After eating the duck, the snake thought my bedroom was just the place for him to go to sleep in and digest his meal; forsnakes, after a hearty meal, always fall into a state of torpor. It was a large python, and it measured—would you believe it?—eighteen feet. Fancy my situation if this fellow had sprung upon me and coiled round me! It would soon have been all over with me. I wonder how long it would have taken to digest me, had I been swallowed by the monster!

One fine day, while walking on the beach of this inhospitable shore, I spied a vessel. It approached nearer and nearer, and at last ran in and hove-to a few miles from the shore. Immediately I observed a gang of slaves rapidly driven down from one of the barracoons. I stood and watched. The men were still in gangs of six, but they had been washed, and each had a clean cloth on. The canoes were immense boats, with twenty-six paddles, and about sixty slaves each. The poor slaves seemed much terrified. They had never been on the rough water before, and they did not know what that dancing motion of the sea was. Then they were being taken away, they knew not whither. As they skimmed over the waves and rolled, now one way, now another, they must have thought their last day had come, and that they were to be consigned to a watery grave.

I was glad that these poor creatures could not see me, for I was hidden from their view by trees and bushes. I felt ashamed of myself—I actually felt ashamed of being a white man! Happily, such scenes are rarely if ever witnessed nowadays, and the slave trade will soon belong to the past.

Two hours afterwards, the vessel, with a cargo of six hundred slaves, was on her way to Cuba.

CHAPTER XV.

GOING INTO THE INTERIOR—SLEEPING WITH THE KING'S RATS—THE CHIMPANZEE—KILL A GAZELLE—TOO COLD TO SLEEP—THE GREY PARTRIDGE.

After this I went again to visit King Bango, and was announced to his Majesty by his great mafouga. I had an important object in paying this visit. I wished to ask the king to permit me to go into the interior and to spare me some people to show me the way.

Bango liked me, though I had declined to marry one of his beautiful daughters. So he granted my request, and gave me twenty-five men, some of whom were reputed great hunters in that country. They had killed many elephants and brought all the ivory to their king. They were the providers of the royal table, and passed their lives in the hunt and in the forest.

We made great preparations for the chase, for game was said to be plentiful. We were to encamp many days in the forest, and to have a jolly time, and a hard time, too, for the hunter's life is not an easy one. I was invited by the king to sleep in his palace, so that the next day I might start early; so I was led to my bedroom by the great mafouga. It was so dirty and gloomy that I wished myself fast asleep under a tree in the forest. I looked around, thinking that perhaps the king wanted to get rid of me, and had invited me there to have me murdered; but finding nothing suspicious, I concluded that old King Bango had never entertained such ideas, and I felt vexed at myself for having such thoughts on my mind. Then I extinguished the light and lay down on the royal couch. I had scarcely lain down when I began to hear a strange noise. At first I did not know what it meant. The noise in the room increased. What could it be? I tried to see through the darkness, but could distinguish nothing. Just then I felt something getting under my blanket. Confounded, I jumped up, not knowing what it might be. It was an enormous rat. As soon as I got up, I heard a perfect scrambling of rats going back where they came from, and then all became silent. I lay down on the bed again and tried to sleep, but in vain, on account of the assaults and gambols of the rats, of which there was a prodigious number. They seemed inclined to dispute possession of my room with me. They were continually on mybed, and running over my face. I soon got quite enough of the royal palace. I wished I had never come into it. But it was an excellent place for getting up early. No sooner had the morning twilight made its appearance than I rose and called my men together; and, though we could hardly see, we set out at once on the march.

I went in advance with Aboko, my head man, and Niamkala, the next best man, at my side. Both these men were great hunters, and had spent the principal part of their lives in the woods. They seemed really like men of the woods, so very wild were their looks. Aboko was a short, somewhat stout man; very black, and extremely muscular, very flat-nosed, and with big thick lips. His eyes were large and cunning, and seemed to wander about; his body bore marks of many scratches from thorny trees and briars; his legs displayed great strength. Niamkala, on the contrary, was tall and slender, not very dark; he had sharp piercing eyes, and seemed to be continually looking after something. Both were first-rate elephant hunters.

Aboko, Niamkala, and I became great friends, for we were all three hunters, and loved the woods.

Our way led through some beautiful prairies, each surrounded by dark forests, and seeming like natural gardens planted in this great woody wilderness. The country was really lovely. The surface was mostly rolling prairie, with a light sandy soil. The highest hills often broke into abrupt precipices, on which we would come suddenly; and if any of us had tumbled down to the bottom, he would never have been heard of again. The woods are the safe retreat of the elephant. Great herds of buffaloes are found there, also antelopes, which go out into the great grass fields by night to play and feed. Leopards are also abundant.

I was much pleased to be able to travel in an open space, and not always through the dark forest The breeze fanned our faces as we went onward. Presently we saw the footprints of huge elephants and of wild buffaloes. Friend Aboko now warned us to look sharp, for we were sure to see game. Sure enough, he had hardly spoken when we saw a bull standing, deer-like, upon the edge of the wood, watching us, I suppose, and no doubt greatly puzzled to make out what kind of animals we were. He stood for some minutes, safe out of range, and then turned into the woods, evidently not liking our appearance. We ran around to intercept him; and I waited at one pass in the woods, for Aboko to go clear around and drive the bull towards me.

I was waiting, when suddenly I saw something approaching me out of the deep gloom of the forest. I thought it was Aboko coming towards me, and I waited anxiously for news. I did not say a word for fear of frightening the game that might be near us. The object came nearer and nearer to me, till I thought I could recognise Aboko's dark face distinctly through the foliage. I stood with my gun resting on the ground, when suddenly I heard a shrill scream, and then what I thought to be Aboko turned and ran back into the woods, showing a broad, big hairy body. It was one of the wild men of the woods—the chimpanzee—and a big one it was, I assure you.

How glad I was to have seen this wild man of the woods! For a few minutes I felt so astonished that I did not move. His black face certainly did look very much like that of an African, so much so that, as I have already said, I took the chimpanzee to be Aboko.

By-and-by the real Aboko made his appearance. This time there was no illusion, and we had a good laugh over my mistake. I felt quite vexed that I hadnot shot the chimpanzee. I should have liked so much to look at the animal closely. But I felt it was almost like shooting a man.

We left the woods, and started once more for the interior. We had not been long on our way when I spied a gazelle right in the middle of the prairie. How could one approach it without being seen? for the grass was short. We wanted very much to kill it, for we had not killed anything yet; and what were we to have for our dinner and supper? No one likes to go without dinner, especially when working hard. Aboko, Niamkala, and I held a council. We lay down flat on the ground for fear of being seen; and finally it was agreed that I should go towards the gazelle with my long range gun and shoot it if I could. So I started. I almost crawled, now and then raising my head just to the level of the grass, to see if the animal was still there. When I thought I was near enough, I quietly lay down flat on the ground and rested my gun on an ant-hill that looked like a mushroom. Taking careful aim at the unsuspicious animal I fired, and down it tumbled, to my great delight. Aboko and Niamkala, who had been watching afar off, came rushing and shouting, their faces beaming with joy. The prospect of a good dinner cheered them up.

Others of the party soon joined us. The gazelle was cut upon the spot, and we continued our journey till we came to a beautiful little stream, which was too deep to be forded. A huge tree had been felled, and we crossed to the other side on it, though it was hard work. I assure you I thought once or twice I should have tumbled into the water.

At sunset we stopped, quite tired out. We made our camp in the midst of the prairie in order to have the nice grass to lie upon. It was the dry season, and we were not afraid of getting wet. The people went intothe nearest forest and collected an immense quantity of firewood, not a difficult task, as so many dead limbs were lying on the ground.

We lighted a great many large fires, which blazed up fiercely, for the wind blew hard. The country around was illuminated, and the glare of our fires must have been seen a long way off. We took our dinner and supper at the same time. I roasted my own share of the gazelle myself; I put a piece of stick through the flesh and laid the skewer across two forked sticks, which I fixed in the ground on each side of the fire. I longed for some lard to baste the roasting meat, but I was thankful for the good dinner I had, and I enjoyed it thoroughly. I had a little bit of salt to eat with it, and also some nice cayenne pepper.

My men also seemed to enjoy their meal very much, for they had meat to their heart's content; and these negroes are very gluttonous generally. It was laughable to see how lazily we lay around on the grass by our fires; some were smoking, others tried to sleep, while others told stories; but we all tried to warm ourselves, and kept continually adding fuel to the already bright fires.

The night was clear and almost frosty. The stars shone brilliantly above our heads, and it was bright moonlight. It became so windy and cold that we regretted we had not encamped by the forest, where we should have been sheltered from the wind. It was too cold to sleep, even with my blanket; and my poor men, who had no blankets, were shivering around the fires.

So at two o'clock in the morning I ordered the men to get up. A couple of hours' sharp walking brought us to a thick wood, and there we were sheltered. We quickly made up one very large fire, big enough for all of us, and stretched ourselves pell-mell aroundit for a short nap. We were so tired that we soon fell asleep, not caring for leopards or anything else. We were awakened by the cry of the grey partridge (*Francolinus squamatus*), called *quani* by the natives.

I will now say a word about these partridges. Unlike our partridges, they perch on trees. When evening comes, the old cock perches himself first, and calls the flock together. They all settle near each other. In the morning, before daylight, they begin to cluck; and it was this noise that we heard. They do not sleep on the ground, like our partridges, because there are too many snakes crawling about, and too many carnivorous animals.

CHAPTER XVI.

THE HIPPOPOTAMUS—A SPECK OF WAR—REACH NGOLA—A SUNDAY TALK—THE BLACK MAN'S GOD AND THE WHITE MAN'S GOD—HOW KING NJAMBAI PUNISHED HIS WIFE—WE BUILD AN OLAKO IN THE WOODS.

Sunrise found us under way again; and before us lay a fine stretch of prairie, on the farther borders of which were quietly grazing several herds of buffaloes, which, as we approached them, quickly ran into the woods. While theyremained in sight they gave the country a civilized appearance; it looked like a large grazing farm in June, with cattle, and hay almost ready for harvest; a fine, quiet, old-country picture here in the wilds of Africa, that reminded me so much of home scenes that I felt happy and elated.

We pushed on rapidly in order to travel as far as possible before the heat of the day should set in. We came to a large pool or lakelet; and, while looking at the water, I suddenly saw something strange coming out from under its surface. It was a hippopotamus—the first I had seen. I thought it was a log of wood; then I fancied it was the head of a horse; for certainly, from a distance, the head of a hippopotamus looks like that of a horse. Then I heard a great grunt, and down went the head under the water. Suddenly a number of the animals made their appearance; there were at least a dozen of them. They began sporting in the water, now popping their huge heads out and snorting, and then diving to the bottom and remaining there for some time.

I watched them for a while, and then I took my gun, intending to send a bullet into the head of one and haul him ashore; but Aboko said they would sink to the bottom. Not wishing to kill one of these creatures for nothing, I took Aboko's advice, and we went away.

We had not met a single human being since we left Sangatanga till now. As we journeyed, I saw in the distance what I at first took to be a herd of buffaloes, but soon perceived it was a caravan of natives coming in our direction. Immediately we looked at our guns; for in this country there is no law, and every man's hand is against his brother. We saw that they, too, prepared for an encounter; that most of them hid in the grass, watching. Four fellows came towards us to reconnoitre, and to ask if it was peace or war, whensuddenly they got a glimpse of me, and I do not know how, but they at once saw, from the fact of my being there, that there would be no war. They shouted to their companions to come and see the Otangani.

They were Shekianis, who, as I have said, are a very warlike people, and this part of the country, I was told, was thickly inhabited by them. We left them in the midst of their wonders, and travelled as fast as we could, for we wanted to reach a village of their tribe, named Ngola, whose chief was a friend of King Bango, and was his vassal, having married one of his daughters.

At last, after much travelling, we reached the village of Ngola. As we approached, and as soon as the women caught sight of me, they ran screaming into the houses. Njambai, the chief, received us very kindly, and gave me a house to live in.

Ngola was a very pretty village, and the house I lived in belonged to Shinshooko, the brother of the chief. You will agree with me that Shinshooko had a funny name. He was a worthy fellow, and tolerably honest, too, for he gave me the key of one of his doors—(I wonder where he got the old padlock that was on it)—and he recommended me to shut my door every time I went away, as the people might steal something.

Sunday came; I remained in the village. They all understood the Oroungou language so I could speak to them. I told them there was no such thing as witchcraft, and that it was very wrong to accuse people of it and kill them; that there was only one God, who made both the whites and the blacks, and we should all love Him. This elicited only grunts of surprise and incredulity. They all shouted that there were two gods,—the God of the *Ntangani* (white men) and the God of the *Alombai* (black men). The God of the black men had never given them anything, while theGod of the white men had sent them guns, powder, and many other fine things. Then Shinshooko remarked, "You have rivers of *alongon* (rum) flowing through your land. When I go to Sangatanga I taste it at King Bango's; how much I should like to live on the banks of such rivers!" They would not believe that we had only rivers of water like theirs; and that we ourselves made our powder, and guns, and rum also.

I stayed for a few days in the village of Ngola, where the people were very kind to me. One day I heard a woman crying out, as if she were in great pain. Asking what was the matter, a man told me the king was punishing one of his wives; and others said that, if I did not go to her help, she might be killed. I hurried to the king's house, and there, in front of the verandah, a spectacle met my eyes, which froze my blood with horror. A woman was tied by the middle to a stout stake driven into the ground. Her legs were stretched out and fastened to other smaller stakes, and stout cords were bound round her neck, waist, ankles, and wrists. These cords were being twisted with sticks; and when I arrived the skin was bursting from the terrible compression. The poor woman looked at me. The king was in a perfect rage; he himself was the chief executioner. His eyes were blood-shot, and his lips were white with foam. I had to be careful in expostulating with the king, for fear that he might kill her at once, in a fit of rage. I walked up, and, taking him by the arm, I asked him for my sake to release the poor woman, and not to kill her. He seemed to hesitate; he did not answer, and went into his house. I threatened to leave if he did not release her. Finally he consented, and said: "Let her loose yourself; I give her to you."

How glad I was! I rushed out immediately and began to untie the savage cords, and to cut them away with my knife. The poor creature was covered with blood. I sent her to my house and took care of her. I learned that she had stolen some of her husband's beads.

After this, I left the Shekiani village of Ngola and went on my journey with my friends, Aboko and Niamkala. We travelled on, till, on reaching a place in the midst of a forest, not far from a little lake, we determined to build an olako; for I liked the country so much that I did not want to leave it. There were a great many wild animals in the neighbourhood, and we thought the place was likely to afford us good sport, especially as the lake would draw beasts down to its banks to drink. We were not only near water, but we had a wide stretch of forest and prairie-land about us. We worked very hard that day, building and arranging our encampment, in such a way as to make everything comfortable and secure. Of course we selected the prettiest part of the forest, and where there were many tall and shady trees. We first cut the underbrush from under the trees, and also many of the vines or creepers, which looked very singular as they hung down over our heads. Then we collected a great number of large leaves, which are called by some tribes *shayshayray* and *guaygayrai*, to roof our sheds with. After this we proceeded to cut a number of small sticks, seven or eight feet long, and began to construct our habitations. Then we cut branches of trees to shield us from the wind, and collected a great quantity of firewood, for we had made up our minds to keep ourselves warm. After we had arranged and lighted the fires, our camp looked quite like a little village. It was very romantic and beautiful. I had arranged my own shelter very nicely; and it was first in the row. To be sure, my bed was rather hard, being composed of sticks and leafy branches; while for a pillow I had merely a piece of wood.

In the midst of our work, ten slaves of Njambai came, laden with provisions, which the good fellow had sent after me. After doing a hard day's work, I think we deserved to rest comfortably in the evening. We began cooking our dinner; and a right good dinner it was. My men had monkey and buffalo-meat; but I had a nice fat fowl, which my friend Njambai had sent me.

Before dinner I warned my men to be honest, and keep their fingers at home. They were good fellows, but I found that all savages will steal. So I threatened to kill the first man I caught meddling with my property, and told them I would shoot without mercy; "and then," said I, with great sternness, "when I have blown your brains out, I will settle the matter with your king." To which Aboko coolly replied that the settlement was not likely to do them any particular good.

Of course they all protested that they were honest; but I knew them better than they knew themselves; I knew the effect of temptation on them, poor fellows! and had more confidence in their faith that I would kill the thief than I had in their good resolutions.

When this little matter was settled, they drew around the blazing fire. By this time, the buffalo-meat suspended in a huge kettle over the fire was cooked and ready to be eaten; the monkeys had been roasted on charcoal; my fowl had been cooked; and before us was a great pile of roasted plantain. We enjoyed a hearty meal together; I eating off a plate, and using a fork, while the black fellows took fresh leaves for plates, and used the "black man's fork," as they call their five fingers. After dinner, they drank a large calabash-full of palm wine that had been brought from Ngola; and then, to crown their feast, with the greatest delight of all, I went to one of myboxes, and, lifting the lid, while the shining black faces peered at me with saucer-eyes of expectation, I took out a huge plug of Kentucky tobacco. There was a wild hurrah of joy from them all. They shouted that I was their friend; they loved only me; they would go with nobody else; I was their good spirit; I was like one of themselves. I distributed the tobacco among them; and in a few minutes all were lying about the fire, or seated round it, with their pipes in their mouths.

After making the fire burn brightly I, being tired, went and lay down, as you see me in the picture. My blanket was the only article of bedding I had; I wrapped this around me, and rested my head on my wooden pillow, which I assure you was not of the softest kind. I felt pleased to see my men so contented. Their wild stories of hunting adventures, of witchcraft, and evil spirits well fitted the rude, picturesque surroundings; and they lay there talking away, till, at last, I was obliged to remind them that it was one o'clock, and time to go to sleep, especially as some of us were to get up very early and go hunting. Then all became silent, and soon we all fell asleep, except the men appointed to keep the fires bright, on account of the leopards, and also to watch that we might not be surprised by some enemy.

CHAPTER XVII.

AN UNSUCCESSFUL HUNT FOR ELEPHANTS—I TAKE AIM AT A BUFFALO—A LEOPARD IN THE GRASS NEAR US—WE SHOOT THE LEOPARD AND HER KITTEN—GREAT REJOICING IN CAMP—WHO SHALL HAVE THE TAIL?—A QUARREL OVER THE BRAINS—THE GUINEA HENS—THE MONKEYS.

Early the next morning, Aboko and I got up. Aboko covered himself with his war fetiches, and also with the fetiches that were to bring good luck, and give him a steady hand. On the middle of his forehead was a yellow spot madewith clay. When he had finished these preparations we started.

Our desire was to kill elephants. We saw plenty of tracks, and we hunted all day long. In many places, to judge by the tracks, the elephants had been only an hour or two before ourselves. But we did not see a single elephant, and I killed only a few monkeys for my men's dinner, as well as a few birds.

We were returning to the camp, rather down-hearted, when I heard the cry of the grey male partridge, of which I have already spoken, calling for his mates to come and perch on the tree he had chosen. We turned back to get a shot, if possible, for they are fine eating. We were just on the edge of the forest; and, as I pushed out into the prairie, suddenly I saw several buffaloes, one of which I made sure of as he stood a little in advance of the rest, where the grass was high enough for a stealthy approach. I immediately put a ball into the barrel that had only shot, so that I might have my two barrels loaded with bullets. Then Aboko and I advanced slowly towards the unconscious bull, which stood a fair mark, and I was about to raise my gun when Aboko made a quick sign to hold still and listen. Aboko, at the same time, breathed as if he were smelling something.

I did not know why it was that Aboko had stopped me, but I knew there must be better game at hand, or some other good reason for his doing so. Perhaps he had heard the footstep of an elephant. I looked at his face, and saw that it appeared anxious.

As we stood perfectly motionless, I heard, at apparently a little distance before us, a low purring sound, which might have been taken, by a careless ear, for the sound of the wind passing through the grass. But to Aboko's quick ear it betokened something else.His face grew very earnest, and he whispered to me "Njego" (leopard).

What were we to do? The noise continued. We cocked our guns, and moved, slowly and cautiously, a few steps ahead, to get a position where we thought we might see over the grass. The leopard might pounce upon us at any moment. What would prevent him from doing so if he chose? Certainly not our guns, for we did not know exactly where the beast was. To tell you the truth, I did not feel comfortable at all; I had a slight objection to being carried away in the jaws of a leopard and devoured in the woods.

Our situation was far from being a pleasant one. The leopard comes out generally by night only, and nothing but extreme hunger will bring him out of his lair in open day. When he is hungry, he is also unusually savage, and very quick in his motions.

We knew the animal was near, but we could not succeed in getting a sight of him. As the wind blew from him towards us, I perceived plainly a strong peculiar odour which this animal gives out; and this fact proved, still more decidedly, that the leopard could not be far off. The thought passed through my mind: Is he watching us? Is he coming towards us—crouching like a cat on the ground, and ready to spring upon us when near enough? Do his eyes penetrate the grass which we cannot see through? If so, is he ready to spring?

Meantime our buffalo-bull stood stupidly before his herd, not twenty yards from us, utterly innocent of the presence of so many of his formidable enemies—the leopard, Aboko, and myself.

Just then we moved a little to one side, and, peering through an opening in the grass, I beheld an immense leopard, a female, with a tiny young leopard by her side. The beast saw us at the same moment, having turned her head quickly at some slight noise we made. She had been watching the buffalo so intently as not to notice our approach. It seemed to me as if a curious look of indecision passed over her face. She, too, had more game than she had looked for, and was puzzled which to attack first. Her long tail swished from side to side, and her eyes glared, as she hesitated for a moment to decide which of the three—the bull, Aboko, or me—to pounce upon and make her victim.

But I saved her the trouble of making up her mind; for, in far less time than it takes me to tell you what took place, I had put a ball into her head, which, luckily for us, relieved her of further care for prey. She dropped down dead. At the same moment Aboko fired into the little leopard and killed it. At the noise of the guns, the buffalo-bull and the herd decamped in the opposite direction, at a tremendous pace, the bull little knowing the circumstances to which he owed his life.

I felt much relieved, for I had never before been in quite so ticklish a situation, and I felt no particular desire ever to be in a similar plight again.

When we returned to the camp there was a great excitement as soon as they heard the news that two leopards had been killed. Aboko carried in the young leopard on his back; but mine was too heavy, and had to be left in the field. Guns were fired in rejoicing; and the big leopard was fetched in. When the people returned with it to the camp, all shouted, "What an enormous beast! what an enormous beast! We heard gun firing," etc., etc.

In the midst of this noise Niamkala made his appearance with some of our party, bringing in some wild boars and a pretty little gazelle which the natives called *ncheri*. Of course the wild boars had been cutup into several pieces, for they were too heavy to carry whole.

Niamkala and his party were received with great cheers. The prospect of a good supper brightened all their faces, and mine also; and I shouted, "Well done, Niamkala and boys!"

Everything was brought to my feet. There was so much to eat that there was no use in dividing the meat into equal shares; so I let everyone take as much as he liked.

After supper the leopards were hung on a pole resting on two forked sticks; and then the negroes danced round them. They sang songs of victory, and exulted over and abused the deceased leopard (the mother). They addressed to her comical compliments upon her beauty (and the leopard is really a most beautiful animal). They said, "What a fine coat you have!" (meaning her skin). "We will take that coat off from you." They shouted, "Now you will kill no more people! Now you will eat no more hunters! Now you cannot leap upon your prey! What has become of the wild bull you were looking after so keenly? Would you not have liked to make a meal of Aboko or of Chaillie?" (for they called me Chaillie).

Thus they sang and danced round till towards morning, when I made them go to sleep.

Next morning there was great quarrelling among my men. What could be the matter? I found that Niamkala was declaring his determination to have the end of my leopard's tail, while the rest of the hunters asserted their equal right to it. Aboko said he did not care, as he would have the tail of the one he had killed.

I skinned the two leopards in the most careful manner, and gave the end of the tail to Niamkala, and I promised Fasiko to give him the tail of the next one I should kill. They all shouted, "I hope you will kill leopards enough to give to each of us a tail!"

Poor Fasiko looked very down-hearted. When I inquired why, he said, "Don't you know that when a man has the end of a leopard's tail in his possession he is sure to be fortunate in winning the heart of the girl he wants to marry?"

I said, "Fasiko, you have one wife, what do you care for a leopard's tail?"

He replied, "I want a good many wives."

The palaver about the tail was hardly over when another quarrel broke out. This time it was about the brains. Aboko, Niamkala, and Fasiko each wanted the whole brain of the animal. The others said they must have some too; that there was only one end to each tail, but that the brains could be divided among them all. For a few minutes a fight seemed imminent over the head of the leopard.

I said, "You may quarrel, but no fighting. If you do you will see me in the fight; and I will hit everybody, and hit hard too." At the same time I pointed out to them a large stick lying by my bedside. This immediately stopped them.

They all wanted the brain, they said, because, when mixed with some other charms, it makes a powerful *monda* (fetiche), which gives its possessors dauntless courage and great fortune in the hunt. Happily, I was able to persuade my three best hunters that they wanted no such means to bolster up their courage.

The dispute over the brains being settled, Aboko, in the presence of all the men, laid the liver before me. As this had no value or interest for me, since I was certainly not going to eat the liver of the leopard for my dinner, I was about to kick it aside, when they stopped me, and entreated me to take off the gall and destroy it, in order to save the party from futuretrouble. These negroes believe the gall of the leopard to be deadly poison, and my men feared to be suspected by their friends or enemies at Sangatanga of having concealed some of this poison. So I took off the gall, put it under my feet and destroyed it, and then, taking the earth in which it had been spilled, I threw it in every direction, for I did not want any of these poor fellows to be accused of a crime, and lose their lives by it. I intended to inform the king, on my return, that we had destroyed the liver. But I told my men that their belief was all nonsense, and a mere superstition. They said it was not. As I could not prove their notion to be false, I stopped the discussion by saying I did not believe it.

Having plenty of game, we carried the leopard-meat a long way off, and threw it away.

We did not go hunting for two days, but spent our time in smoking the meat we had on hand. It was just the sort of weather for hunting, and for living in the woods. The air was cool and refreshing, for it was June, and the dry season; but the sky was often clouded, which prevented the sun from being oppressive. To add to our pleasure, the forest trees were in bloom, and many of them were fragrant. The nights were very cold indeed for this country, the thermometer going down to sixty-eight degrees Fahrenheit. The wind blew hard, but against that we managed to protect ourselves. The dews were not nearly so heavy as they are in the rainy season. The grass was in great part burned off the prairies.

Every day we succeeded in shooting more or less game, among which were antelopes, gazelles, wild boars, monkeys without number, and guinea fowls. These guinea fowls were of a beautiful species. In this country you have never seen any like them.

My joy was great when I killed this hitherto unknown species of guinea-fowl (*Numida plumifera*). It is one of the handsomest of all the guinea-fowls yet discovered. Its head is naked, the skin being of a deep bluish-black tinge, and is crowned with a beautiful crest of straight, erect, narrow, downy feathers, standing in a bunch close together. The plumage of the body is of a fine bluish-black ground, variegated with numerous *eyes* of white, slightly tinged with blue. The bill and legs are coloured a blue-black, similar to the skin of the head.

This bird is not found near the seashore. It is very shy, but marches in large flocks through the woods. At night they perch on trees, where they are protected from the numerous animals which prowl about.

I killed several beautiful monkeys called by the natives *mondi*. What curious-looking monkeys they were! Only the stuffed specimen of a young one had been received in England before this time. The mondi is entirely black, and is covered with long shaggy hair. It has a very large body, and a funny little head, quite out of proportion to the size of the animal. It is a very beautiful monkey; the hair is of a glossy jet black; and it has a very long tail. In Africa no monkeys have prehensile tails; I mean by that, tails which they can twist round the branch of a tree, and so hang themselves with the head downwards. That kind of monkey is only found in South America.

The mondi has a dismal cry, which sounds very strangely in the silent woods, and always enabled me to tell where these monkeys were.

CHAPTER XVIII.

ALONE IN CAMP—HUNTING FOR ELEPHANTS—ABOKO KILLS A ROGUE ELEPHANT—I CUT ANOTHER PYTHON IN TWO—WE SHOOT SOME WILD BOARS—A BUFFALO HUNT—RETURN TO SANGATANGA—KING BANGO SICK.

One fine day I remained in the camp, for I had been hunting so much that I wanted a day of rest. All the others had gone to hunt. I was left alone, and I enjoyed the solitude, everything around me was so beautiful and quiet. Nature seemed to smile on all sides. I placed myself at the foot of a large tree, and wrote in my journals; and then I thought of the dear friends I had at home, and wondered if they sometimes thought of me. Then I called to mind all I had seen in the wonderful country which I had explored. I could hardly believe it myself: it seemed like a dream. What extraordinary people, and what curious beasts, had I not met!How many wonderful dangers I had escaped! How kind God had been in protecting me! How He had watched over the poor lonely traveller, and taken care of him during sickness! Thus my heart went up in gratitude, and I silently implored that the protection of God might still be granted me.

Towards sunset, Aboko and Niamkala made their appearance, and brought a fine young boar with them. As usual, without saying a word, they came right to me, and put the dead animal at my feet. Then, seating themselves and clapping their hands, Aboko began to tell me what had happened from the time they started in the morning until the time they returned. They forgot nothing, even mentioning the tracks of the animals they had seen. They reported they had found fresh elephant tracks, and thought the elephants had made their head-quarters there for a few days. After hearing this, we immediately resolved that we would all turn out after elephants on the following day.

Accordingly, in the evening, we cleaned and prepared our guns, and everybody went to sleep early.

The next morning we started about daybreak, each of us carrying some provisions. We were to fire no guns in the forest, for fear of frightening the elephants, who are very shy in this region. We had taken pains to load our guns in the most careful manner.

We hunted all day, but in vain; no elephants were to be seen. We slept out in the woods, for we were too far from the camp to return. We felt so tired that we had only sufficient strength left to enable us to fetch firewood, and to cut a few branches of trees and lie down upon them. I had lost or forgotten the matches, so I had to light the fire with a piece of steel and a gun-flint. This took a little longer.

Very soundly we all slept, as you may easily suppose. When I awoke in the midst of the night our fires were almost out; at least they did not blaze up enough to frighten the wild beasts. Aboko, Niamkala, and Fasiko were snoring tremendously. One was lying flat on his back, the other had his legs up, while Fasiko had his arm extended at full length. By the side of each was his gun, which touched him in some way, so that it could not be taken without awaking him. I believe it was their snoring that had aroused me. They were so tired, and seemed to sleep so soundly, that I did not want to wake them, so I went and added fuel to the fire, which soon began to blaze up again.

The next day found us again exploring the woods in every direction. Elephants certainly were not plentiful; besides they travelled much in search of their favourite food—a kind of fern, which was not very abundant. Again I got very tired; but at last, in the afternoon, we came across our quarry.

Emerging from a thick part of the forest into a prairie which bordered it, we saw to our left, just upon the edge of the wood, a solitary bull elephant. There we stood still. I wonder what he was thinking about! I had seen the great beast in menageries, and also among the Fans, and I have described to you an elephant hunt in their country, but then there was great confusion.

Here, the huge animal stood quietly by a tree, innocent of our presence; and now, for the first time in my life, I was struck with the vast size of this giant of the forests. Large trees seemed like small saplings when compared with the bulk of this immense beast which was standing placidly near them.

What were we to do but to kill him? Though I felt a sense of pity at trying to destroy so noble an animal, yet I was very anxious to get the first shot myself; for it was a "rogue elephant"—that is, an elephant unattached. It was an old one, as we could see by the great size of its tusks. I remembered that rogue elephants are said to be very ferocious. So much the better, I thought. I had killed a good deal of game, and I had ceased to be afraid of any of them, though I felt that hunting was no child's play.

Sir Emerson Tennent ("Ceylon," vol. ii. p. 304) speaks of "the class of solitary elephants, which are known by the term of *Goondapo*, in India, and from their vicious propensities, and predatory habits, are called Hora, or Rogues, in Ceylon."

You must not think that we were standing up all this time in sight of the elephant. As soon as we had seen him, we lay down and hid ourselves in the forest, in such a manner as not to lose sight of him. Then we held a grand council, and talked over what must be done to bag the beast.

The grass was burnt in every direction to the leeward of him, and we dared not risk approaching him from the windward for fear he should smell us. What was to be done? The eyes of my men were fixed upon me with a keenly inquisitive look. They expected me to tell them what I thought best to do about the matter.

I looked at the country, and saw that the grass was very short; and, after taking account of all the chances of approach, I was compelled to admit that I could not manage to get near the beast myself with any certainty. I could not crawl on the ground; my clothes were sure to be seen by the elephant; therefore, as a sensible hunter, I was reluctantly compelled to resign in favour of Aboko, who, I thought, was the best man for the difficult undertaking. His eyes glistened with pleasure as he thought that now he could show his skill. Besides, among hunters there is something pleasant and exciting in knowing that you are about to rush into danger.

After cocking his musket, Aboko dropped down in the short grass, and began to creep up to the elephant slowly on his belly. The rest of us remained where we had held our council, and watched Aboko as he glided through the grass for all the world like a huge boa-constrictor; for, from the slight glimpses we caught, his back, as he moved farther and farther away from us, resembled nothing so much as the folds of a great serpent winding his way along. Finally we could no longer distinguish any motion. Then all was silence. I could hear the beating of my heart distinctly, I was so excited.

The elephant was standing still, when suddenly the sharp report of a gun rang through the woods and over the plain, and elicited screams of surprise from sundry scared monkeys who were on the branches of a tree close by us. I saw the huge beast helplessly tottering till he finally threw up his trunk, and fell in a dead mass at the foot of a tree. Then the black body of Aboko rose; the snake-like creature had become a man again. A wild hurrah of joy escaped from us; I waved my old hat, and threw it into the air, and we all made a run for the elephant. When we arrived, there stood Aboko by the side of the huge beast, calm as if nothing had happened, except that his body was shining with sweat. He did not say a word, but looked at me, and then at the beast, and then at me again, as if to say: "You see, Chaillu, you did right to send me. Have I not killed the elephant?"

The men began to shout with excitement at such a good shot. "Aboko is a man," said they, as we looked again at the beast, whose flesh was still quivering with the death agony. Aboko's bullet had entered his head a little below the ear, and, striking the brain, was at once fatal.

Aboko began to make fetich-marks on the groundaround the body. After this was done we took an axe, which Fasiko had carried with him, and broke the skull, in order to get out the two tusks, and very large tusks they were.

Of course we could not carry off the elephant, so Aboko and I slept that night near our prize on the grass and under the tree. Niamkala and Fasiko had started for the camp to tell the men the news, and the next morning all the men hurried out. While quietly resting under the shade of a tree close to the elephant, I spied them coming. As soon as they recognised us they shouted, and, when near enough, they made a spring at Aboko and then at the elephant. All the cutlasses, all the axes and knives that were in the camp, had been sharpened and brought out. Then the cutting up of the elephant took place. He was not very fat. What a huge beast he was! What a huge liver he had! What an enormous heart, too!

The trunk, being considered a choice morsel, was cut into small pieces. The meat was to be smoked immediately, and then carried to Sangatanga, to be sold and given away. Great bargains were looming before the men's eyes; they were all to get rich by selling the elephant's meat.

I never saw men more happy than these poor fellows were. The negroes believe in eating. Mine ate nothing but meat, and they ate such quantities of it that several of them got sick, and I was obliged to give them laudanum in brandy to cure them. They almost finished my little stock of brandy.

The camp was full of meat, and as we had no salt, the odour that came from it was not particularly agreeable. Indeed, I had to have a separate shanty built on one side, and to the windward of the camp. I could not stand the stench.

At night the negroes lay around the fires, the jolliestof mortals, drinking palm-wine, which they made regularly from the neighbouring palm-trees, and smoking tobacco when I was generous enough to give them some. In fact, they were as honest a set of negroes as I had met with anywhere, really good fellows.

As time passed on you must not think that I did nothing but kill animals. I rambled through the forest, and studied everything I saw. Sometimes, when too far away from the camp, and after a day of hard hunting, I slept soundly under a tree by the side of a big fire, with my gun by my side. I thought I would go hunting one day for wild animals; on another, for birds; and, when too tired to travel, I would remain in the camp, sleeping sweetly on my primitive couch, which consisted of a couple of mats spread on the bare and soft earth, with a thick blanket for cover, the foliage of a tree and the blue starlit sky being my canopy and roof. I had given up sleeping upon bare sticks, finding it too hard.

As fresh boar tracks had been seen near the camp, I could not resist the temptation of having another hunt after that savage beast. However tired I might be, I could hardly keep still whenever news came that game was near us. I was always in the hope of finding some new animal or something curious to stuff and bring home, to show what I had done.

We had not gone far when we heard, to the right of us, the grunting of some wild boars. As they are very wild, we jumped hastily behind a fallen tree to hide ourselves. In our haste to do this, I heedlessly stepped on something in my path, and, looking down, found I was running upon an immense serpent, a huge python, which lay snugly coiled up beside the tree. Happily, he was in a state of stupefaction, consequent, probably, on having eaten too heavy a dinner. Hescarcely moved, and did not raise his head. I ran to Niamkala, and borrowed a kind of heavy cutlass which he carried with him, and with a blow of this I cut the python in two pieces, which instantly began to squirm about in a very snaky and horrible way. During his death-struggle the monster disgorged the body of a young gazelle, which was in a half digested condition. This python was not quite twenty feet long—a pretty good-sized one, you may judge.

The noise we made in killing the snake of course frightened the wild pigs. We pursued them, and succeeded, by good management, and after a hard chase of an hour, in coming up with the herd. They were ten in number, and we managed to bag two. They were not very large. Besides these pigs, my hunters carried the two halves of the serpent to the camp. We were received there with demonstrations of joy. They made a kind of soup with the boa, and seemed to relish it very much. I did not taste it, and can therefore say nothing against it.

I never saw a country like this for game. There was so much prairie land that it reminded me of Southern Africa. The contrast with the great forest, where I had travelled for days without seeing anything, was very great.

For a few days I remained quiet in the camp. The men had in the meantime been hunting and exploring in various directions. As they reported that great herds of buffaloes frequented every night a prairie situated about ten miles from our camp, I determined to have a hunt for them. I was very fond of buffaloes, at least of their meat.

We set out and left our camp just before sunset. Our route was through the midst of prairie land, and by eight o'clock in the evening we reached the forest beyond. There we hoped to find our game; andsecuring for ourselves safe hiding-places in the woods on the edge of the plain, we lay down and waited. Now, waiting is generally tedious, but waiting in a cold night from eight to two o'clock, every moment expecting that which does not come, is apt to try one's patience severely. Mine was entirely gone, and I wished myself comfortably under my blanket in camp, when suddenly the buffaloes came. Aboko heard them coming, and presently a herd of about twenty-five animals emerged from the woods, and scattered quietly about the grassy plain.

The moon was going down, and we could see from our hiding-places the long shadows of the buffaloes, silently gliding one way or another, but never near enough to us for a shot. Soon they felt quite at ease, and began feeding, ever and anon gambling sportively with one another. Seeing them engaged, we crawled towards them slowly and with great care. We had almost got within safe range when a sudden change of wind discovered us to them. They snuffed up the air suspiciously, and instantly gathering together, they disappeared in the woods.

There was ill luck! My hunters cursed in Shekiani, and I grumbled in several languages. But there was still hope. Silently we crawled back to our lair, and waited patiently for two mortal hours; when at last two—a bull and a cow—stalked leisurely into the fields and began to crop the grass. It was now dark. The moon had gone down, leaving us only the uncertain light of the stars. We watched the motions of the buffaloes until we thought we could venture, and then silently crawled towards them again. This time we got within range. I chose the bull for my shot, and Niamkala took the cow, while Aboko was ready to second me with his gun in case I should not kill my animal. We fired both at once, and by good luck, forthe light was not enough to afford a chance for a fair shot, both the animals fell down dead.

Daylight soon appeared, and we resolved to return to the camp and send men to bring in the meat, thinking that no wild beasts would trouble our prizes at such unseasonable hours. Aboko and Niamkala first cut off the bushy tails of black glossy hair, and then we made for the camp, where they showed to our companions these trophies of our chase. The men made haste, and reached the place early, but not before the cow was half eaten by a hungry leopard. The poor leopard who ventured out so early in the morning must have been nearly famished. I did not grudge him his meal, though I should have liked to watch for him and shoot him, had I thought of his coming, for I had plenty of friends to whom I could have given his skin on my return.

A few days afterwards we broke up our camp, and loaded ourselves with the birds and beasts I had killed and prepared, and also with the meat which my men had smoked; and all the time they were boasting of how much tobacco and other dainties they would get for this. They seemed very jolly, though groaning under their burdens; and I was pleased to see them so happy. The specimens of the *Bos brachicheros* were an inconvenient load, and I was obliged to be very careful with them.

When I reached Sangatanga I found that the king was in worse health than he was when I had left. He was alarmed, fearing he would die. He remarked that it was singular he had been taken worse immediately after my departure; and that, in fact, he grew sick on the very night when I slept in his house.

CHAPTER XIX.

A JOLLY EXCURSION PARTY—A RACE FOR THE FISHING BANKS—THE OROUNGOU BURIAL-GROUND.

Not long after we returned from our hunting expedition, I prepared to go to Fetich Point on a fishing excursion. For this purpose it was necessary to have canoes. I had called on King Bango since I returned, but, remembering the rats, I had respectfully declined the hospitality of his palace. Nevertheless, he remained my friend and gave me all the men I wanted.

I not only wanted to fish, but I also wished to seethe burial-ground of the Oroungous, which is not far from Fetich Point. There were also some enormous turtles on Fetich Point, I was told, and I wished to catch some of them.

My old hunting friend, Fasiko, had got together a party of forty men. Besides Fetich Point, I was to visit the Fetich river, and the end of Cape Lopez. There being no houses whatever there, the women had prepared for us a great quantity of powdered manioc, baskets of ground nuts, sweet potatoes, and bunches of plantain. We had a very large outfit. Fasiko got together a lot of mats to sleep upon, and kettles to cook in, and a great quantity of salt, with which to salt the fish we hoped to catch. We had several fish-nets made, of the fibre of a vine. We also had fish-hooks; and I took an enormous hook to catch sharks. I always had a hatred of sharks, they are such savage and voracious monsters.

We had a great number of baskets. The women carried these to put the fish in. We did not forget guns; for leopards lurk in the jungle, on the south side of the cape, and the boa hangs from the trees, waiting for his prey. If you got up early there, as everybody at a watering-place should, you can see huge elephants trotting down along the beach, and cooling their tender toes in the surf.

It was a very jolly party, for Cape Lopez is the Cape May, or Nahant of Sangatanga. The dry season there answers to our July, when "everybody that is anybody" is supposed to be "out of town and down by the seaside."

Niamkala and Aboko were of the party; for we were great friends; and wherever I went they wanted to go with me. They were slaves of King Bango; but we had shared the same dangers, we had shared the same pleasures.

At last everything was ready. I embarked in the biggest canoe, which was manned by sixteen oarsmen. As usual, there was a good deal of shouting and bustle before we got off. The sails, made with matting, were unfurled, and we set out across the bay. We had an exciting race to see which canoe was the fastest. There was a stiff *breeze*; but unfortunately the wind was nearly in our faces, so that our sails were of little use. The men worked lustily at their paddles, and as they paddled they sang their wild canoe songs. The morning was clear and bright, but in the afternoon the sky became clouded. We reached Fetich Point a little before sunset; and the men, who seemed as lively and jolly as could be, at once cast their net, in a way not materially different from our mode of using the hand-net, and made a great haul of fish, the principal part of which were mullets. How beautiful they looked! They seemed like silver fish.

The men went immediately in search of firewood. We lighted our fires; and, having cooked and eaten our fish, which were delicious, we prepared for a night's rest by spreading mats upon the sand. It was terribly cold; for we were not sheltered from the wind, which went right through my blanket.

Not far from Fetich Point is the river Tetica, one of the tributaries of the Nazareth river. The Nazareth falls into the bay, through a tangled, dreary, and poisonous track of back country, consisting of mangrove swamps, like those I have described on the Monda river, and where, I daresay, no animals, except serpents, are to be found. There are no human habitations there.

In the morning, I wished to see the Oroungou burial-ground, before starting for Cape Lopez itself. It lay about a mile from our camp, towards Sangatanga, from which it is distant about half a day's pull in a canoe.

It was only by the promise of a large reward that I persuaded Niamkala to accompany me. The negroes visit the place only on funeral errands, and hold it in the greatest awe, conceiving that here the spirits of their ancestors wander about, and that they are not lightly to be disturbed.

Niamkala and I left the camp, and, following the seashore, we soon reached the place. It is in a grove of noble trees, many of them of magnificent size and shape. As I have said, the natives hold the place in great reverence.

The grove is by the sea. It is entirely cleared of underbrush; and, as the wind sighs through the dense foliage of the trees, and whispers in their darkened, somewhat gloomy recesses, there is something awful about the place. I thought how many lives had been sacrificed on these graves.

Niamkala stood in silence by the strand, while I entered the domain of the Oroungou dead.

The corpses are not put below the surface. They lie about beneath the trees, in huge wooden coffins, many of which are made of trees. By far the greater number were crumbling away. Some new ones betokened recent arrivals. The corpses of some had only been surrounded by a mat. Here was a coffin falling to pieces, and disclosing a grinning skeleton within. On the other side were skeletons, already without their covers, which lay in the dirt beside them. Everywhere were bleached bones, and mouldering remains. It was curious to see the brass anklets and bracelets, in which some Oroungou maiden or wife had been buried, still surrounding her whitened bones, and to note the remains of articles which had been laid in the coffin or put by the side of some wealthy fellow now crumbling to dust. What do you think these articles were? Umbrellas, guns, spears, knives, bracelets, bottles, cooking-pots, swords, plates, jugs, glasses, etc.

In some places there remained only little heaps of shapeless dust, from which some copper, or iron, or ivory ornaments, or broken pieces of the articles I have just mentioned, gleamed out, to prove that here, too, once lay a corpse, and exemplifying the saying of the Bible, "Dust, to dust thou shalt return." I could not help saying to myself. "Man, what art thou?"

Suddenly I came to a corpse that must have been put there only the day before. The man looked asleep, for death does not show its pallor in the face of the negro as it does in that of the white man. This corpse had been dressed in a coat, and wore a necklace of beads. By his side stood a jar, a cooking-pot, and a few other articles, which his friend, or his heir, had put by his side.

Passing on into a yet more sombre gloom, I came at last to the grave of old King Pass-all, the brother of the present king. Niamkala had pointed out to me the place where I should find it. The huge coffin lay on the ground, and was surrounded on every side with great chests, which contained some of the property of his deceased majesty. Many of them were tumbling down, and the property destroyed. The wood, as well as the goods, had been eaten up by the white ants. Among some of these chests, and on the top of them, were piled huge earthenware jugs, glasses, mugs, plates, iron pots, and brass kettles. Iron and copper rings, and beads were scattered around, with other precious things which Pass-all had determined to carry to the grave with him. There lay also the ghastly skeletons of the poor slaves, who, to the number of one hundred, were killed when the king died, that he might not pass into the other world without due attendance.

It was a grim sight, and one which filled me with a sadder feeling than even the disgusting slave barracoons had given me.

The land breeze was blowing when I returned, and we started for the sandy point of the cape. It is a curious beach, very low, and covered with a short scrub, which hides a part of the view, while the sand ahead is undistinguishable at a distance from the water, above which it barely rises. I was repeatedly disappointed, thinking we had come to the end, when in fact we had before us a long narrow sand-spit. Finally we reached the extreme end, and landed in smooth water on the inside of the spit.

The point gains continually upon the sea. Every year a little more sand appears above the water, while the line of short shrubs, which acts as a kind of dam or breakwater, is also extended, and holds the new land firm against the encroachments of old Neptune.

Among these shrubs we built our camp, and here for some days we had a very pleasant and lively time.

The weather was delightful; we had no rain, it being the dry season, and we were not afraid of the awful tornadoes.

CHAPTER XX.

OUR CAMP AT POINT FETICH—AN AFRICAN WATERING-PLACE—FISHING, BUT NOT BATHING—THE SHARKS—CURING MULLETS, ETC.—TURNING TURTLES—BIRD SHOOTING—A LEOPARD SPRINGS UPON US.

Our camp presented a very picturesque appearance, and was unlike the one described a little while ago, and of which I gave you a picture. Here each man had built for himself a cosy shade with mats, which, by the way, are very beautiful. These mats are about five or six feet inlength and three feet wide. We made our walls of them, so that we were sheltered from the wind. Our houses looked very much like large boxes.

As usual, the first day was occupied in making everything comfortable, and in collecting firewood, which it was not so easy a matter to find, for the shrubs did not furnish much, and we had to go far to get it; afterwards it was made the business of the children to gather brushwood for the fires; and the poor children had hard work too.

We built large *oralas*, or frames, on which to dry the fish when salted, or to smoke it by lighting a fire beneath, in which case the oralas were built higher.

Some had brought with them large copper dishes, called Neptunes, which looked like gigantic plates, in which they were to boil down salt water to get supplies of salt for salting the fish, and to take home with them. Some of the women were all day making salt; when made, it was packed securely in baskets, and placed near the fire to keep it dry.

Every day we had some new kind of fish to eat, or to salt down.

As for myself, as I have said, I had brought along an immense shark-hook and a stout rope. The hook was attached to a strong chain two feet long, so that the teeth of the shark could not cut the line if they should swallow the piece of meat or the large fish put on the hook for a bait.

There were so many sharks swarming in the waters about the cape that they were often almost washed upon the beach by the waves. I never saw such an immense number. The Chinese, who eat sharks' fins, would find enough here to glut the Canton market. In truth, I sometimes trembled when in a canoe at the idea that it might upset, for if that had happened, in a short time I should have been seized by a dozenhungry sharks, been dragged to the bottom of the sea, and there been devoured. These sharks are certainly the lions and tigers of the water: they show no mercy. The very sight of them is horrible, for you cannot help thinking and saying to yourself, "I wonder how many people this shark has eaten!" There is a superstition among sailors that whenever there is a sick person aboard, the sharks will follow the ship, watching for the corpse to be thrown overboard.

I confess I felt a hatred for sharks, and while at Cape Lopez I killed as many of them as I could. Almost every day you could have seen me in a canoe near the shore, throwing my shark-hook into the sea, and after awhile making for the beach, and calling all the men together to pull with all our might, and draw in my victim. One day I took a blue-skin shark. He was a tremendous fellow. I thought we should never be able to haul him ashore, or that the line would part. It took us an hour before we saw him safely on the beach. Now and then I thought he would get the better of us, and that we should have to let the line go, or be pulled into the water. At last he came right up on the beach, and a great shout of victory welcomed him. Aboko was ready for him, and with a powerful axe he gave him a tremendous blow that cut off his tail. Then we smashed his head, and cut his body into several pieces, which quivered to and fro for some time. In his stomach we found a great number of fish. If I remember correctly, he had six or seven rows of teeth, and such ugly teeth! I pity the poor man whose leg should unfortunately get caught between them.

Hardly a day passed that I did not catch some sharks, and then for a bait I used to put on my hook a piece of their own flesh, which, like the cannibals, they ate apparently without any remorse.

There is another species of shark, of a grey leadencolour, which is shorter and thicker than the blue-skin shark; it has a broader head, and a much wider mouth, and is far more voracious. This species is the most common. It will attack a man in shallow water. I remember a poor boy who was going to his canoe, where the water was not up to his knees, when suddenly, just as he was going to get in, he was seized by his leg and dragged into the water by one of these terrible sharks, which had probably been for some time swimming along the beach watching for prey. In that country it is dangerous to bathe in the sea, and I did not attempt to do so. So much for the sharks.

Every day, on the muddy banks near the mouth of the Fetich river, we hauled in with our nets a great quantity of mullets and other fish. These were split open, cleaned, salted, dried, and smoked, and then packed away in baskets.

Sometimes, early in the morning, we went out to turn turtles. To do this we had to start before daylight. They came on the beach to lay their eggs in the sand, which the sea does not reach. There the heat of the sun hatches them out. I have sometimes spied these turtles early in the morning coming out of the water and ascending the beach in a clumsy way, until they reached the dry spot where they wish to lay their eggs. After laying them, they manage to cover them with sand. I should have liked very much to have seen the young ones come out of the eggs. How funny the little wee turtles must look! But I have never been so fortunate.

One day we caught a turtle which had only three legs; the fourth had been bitten off, no doubt by a hungry shark. The wound had got well, and must have been made long before we caught the turtle.

Would you like to know how we captured turtles?

As soon as they see people coming towards themthey generally make for the water. Then we rush with all speed upon the unwieldy turtle, and with one jerk roll it over on its back, where it lies, vainly struggling to recover its legs. Then we kill it.

Hundreds of eggs are sometimes found in one turtle. I was very fond of them when found in the body, otherwise I did not like them. They made splendid omelettes.

The turtles look very curious when they lie fast asleep on the water. At such times I am told that, with great care, they may be approached and captured.

Besides fishing, we had hunting also. South of the cape was a dense forest, in which might be found most of the animals that live in African woods. Several times we saw elephants on the beach, but we shot none. I killed a great number of sea fowls, which fly about there in such flocks as almost to darken the air. They collect in this way in order to feed on the fish which are so plentiful.

One evening, as Aboko, Niamkala, and I were returning from a fruitless hunt in the woods, we fell in with larger game. Passing along the edge of the forest we were suddenly startled by a deep growl. Looking quickly about, we perceived an immense male leopard just crouching for a spring upon our party. Fortunately our guns were loaded with ball. No doubt we had come upon the animal unawares. In a flash we all three fired into the beast, for there was no time to be lost. He was already upon the spring, and our shot met him as he rose. He fell dead and quivering almost within a foot of Aboko, who may be said to have had a very narrow escape, for the leopard had singled him out as his prey. He was an immense animal, and his skin, which I preserved as a trophy, is most beautifully shaded and spotted; in fact there is scarcely a more beautiful animal than the African leopard.

At the mouth of the Nazareth the savage saw-fish is found. It is no doubt one of the most formidable, and the most terrible of the animals that live in the water.

I was quietly paddling in a little canoe, when my attention was drawn to a great splashing of water a little way off. I saw at once it was a deadly combat between two animals. All round the water was white with foam. The cause of this could not be two hippopotami fighting, for in that case I should have seen them.

I approached cautiously, having first made my two rifles ready in case of an emergency. At last I came near enough to see an enormous saw-fish attacking a large shark. It was a fearful combat; both fought with desperation. But what could the shark do against the powerful saw of his antagonist?

At last they came too near my canoe. I moved off lest they might attack my canoe, for they would have made short work of my small, frail boat; and a single blow of the saw-fish would have disabled me. Each tooth of the saw must have been two inches long, and there were, I should say, forty on each side; the saw was about five feet long. In the end, the saw-fish, more active than the shark, gave him a terrible blow, making his teeth go right through the flesh of the shark. Several such blows were quickly delivered, and all became still, the foam ceased, and the water resumed its accustomed stillness. I paddled towards the scene, when suddenly I saw, at the bottom of the river, what I recognised to be a great shark; it was dead, and lay on its back, showing its belly. The body was frightfully lacerated.

The saw-fish had killed its antagonist, and left the field of battle, and only the blood of the shark stained the water.

In the bay of Cape Lopez, in the month of July, Icould see whales playing about in every direction, and sending water high into the air.

They come at that time of the year with their young; and the water of the bay being very quiet, they enjoy there the sea, and the young whales get strong before they go into the broad ocean. Very pretty it looks to see them swimming by the side of the big mothers.

Year after year the whales came, always in July; but one year the whalers found them out, and made war upon them; and now, when July comes, they are no more to be seen, for the whale is very intelligent, and knows well the places where he is not safe; so they look out for some other unfrequented bay wherein to play and train their young.

Besides the whale, all the year round can be seen what the sailor commonly calls the *bottle-nose*, an enormous fish, not so big as a whale, but nevertheless of great size. It is of the whale family.

CHAPTER XXI.

BOUND FOR THE INTERIOR—A SEA VOYAGE—A TORNADO—
WE REACH THE FERNAND-VAZ—SANGALA WISHES TO
DETAIN ME—A NIGHT ALARM—PROSPECT OF A WAR—
ARRAYED FOR BATTLE—A COMPROMISE—MY COMMI
FRIENDS.

I have been a great wanderer. On the 5th of February, 1857, I was on board
of a little schooner, of forty-five tons burden, bound for the mouth of a
river called Fernand-Vaz. Fromthere I expected to penetrate into the
interior. I was on my way to a wild and unexplored region.

The name of the schooner was the Caroline. She was full of provisions and
goods for the long journey I had to undertake; for I intended to make a
very long exploration before my return to America. The captain was a
Portuguese negro, Cornillo by name. The crew, seven in number, were
Mpongwes, Mbingos, and Croomen, not more than two of whom could
understand each other, and not a soul could properly understand the
captain. A fine prospect for the voyage!

I got aboard at daylight, and should have been glad to go immediately
ashore again; but, by dint of steady shouting, and a great deal of standing
idle, with a little work now and then, we got the anchor up just at dusk. The
captain did not like to leave port on Friday. I told him I would take the
responsibility. He asked what good that would do him if he went to the
bottom. It appears that the Portuguese have the same absurd superstitions
as many of the sailors of other nations.

No sooner had we got into the swell than our two black women, and every
man on board (except the captain), got sea-sick. The cook was unable to
get the breakfast next morning; and the men were lying about, looking like
dying fish.

We set sail from the Gaboon river, and hoped to get down to the Commi
country in five days. But for four days after starting we had light wind and a
contrary current; and, on the fifth day, we were caught in such a storm at
sea as I hope never to experience again.

The steering went on so badly when Captain Cornillo was below, that I was
forced to stand watch myself. I had been steering for four hours, and had
been perhaps one hour in my berth, when I was awakened from a sound
sleep by the captain's voice, giving orders totake down the mainsail. I
sprang on deck immediately, knowing there must be at least a heavy squall
coming. But no sooner did I cast my eyes to the leeward than I saw how
imminent the danger was. A tornado was coming down upon us. The black

clouds which had gathered about the horizon were becoming lurid white with startling quickness. It seemed almost as if they were lit up by lightning. The tornado was sweeping along and in a moment would be upon us. As yet all was still—still as death. There was not a breath of wind.

I turned to see if the mainsail was down, but found nothing had been done. The captain was shouting from the wheel; the men were also shouting and running about, half scared to death; and, in the pitchy darkness (for I could not see my hands when held close before my eyes), no one could find the halliards. In the midst of our trouble the wind came roaring down upon us. I seized a knife, determined to cut everything away; but just then somebody let go the halliards, and, in the nick of time, the mainsail came half-way down. The tornado was upon us. The jibs flew away in rags in a moment. The vessel was thrown upon her beam ends. The water rushed over her deck, and the men sang out that we were drowning; as, in fact, we should have been in a very few minutes. Happily the wind shifted a little; and, by the light of some very vivid lightning, we seized on the mainsail, like men that felt it was their last hope, and pulled it down, holding it so that the wind should not catch it again. The vessel righted, and in less than twenty minutes the squall died away, and was succeeded by a driving rain, which poured down in such torrents that in a very short time I was drenched to the skin. The lightning and thunder were something terrific. I was afraid of the lightning, striking us as the Caroline hadno lightning-rod, and we had powder enough on board to blow us all to atoms. The deck was so leaky that even below I could not get protection from the rain.

The next morning we had no jibs, and our other sails were severely damaged. To add to our difficulties, no one on board, not even our captain, knew where we were. At that time I knew not how to make astronomical observations. The captain was in the habit of bringing up, every day, an old quadrant; but about the use of it he knew as much as a cow does about a musket.

At last we made the land. A canoe came on board, and we asked where we were. We found that we must be somewhere near Cape St. Catherine, and therefore a good many miles south of the mouth of the Fernand-Vaz, the place where I was bound. So we turned about to retrace our path. Sailing close in shore, when I passed the village of Aniambia, or Big Camma, the natives came with a message from their king, offering me two slaves if I would stay with him.

I was immovable, for I had set my heart on going to the Fernand-Vaz river, of which I heard a good deal, from my friend Aboko, while in the Cape Lopez regions. As we approached that river, the vast column of water, pushing seaward, forced its separate way through the ocean for at least four or five miles; and the water there was almost fresh, and seemed a separate current in the sea.

At last we came to the mouth of the Fernand-Vaz, and our fame had gone before us. Some of the Commi people, the inhabitants of the Fernand-Vaz, had seen me before at Cape Lopez. The news had spread that I wanted to settle at the village of a chief called Ranpano; so, as we passed his seashore village, a canoe came off to ask me to land; but as the breakers were rather formidable, I begged to be excused.

Ranpano's men wanted much to hug me; and were so extravagant in their joy, that I had to order them to keep their hands off, their shining and oily bodies having quite soiled my clothes. They went back to the king to tell him the good news. I kept one of these men on board for a pilot, being now anxious to get across the intricate bar, and fairly into the river, before dark.

As we sailed along up the river, canoes belonging to different villages shot out to meet us; and presently I had a crowd alongside anxious to come on board, and sufficient almost to sink us. They took me for a slaver at first, and their joy was unbounded; for there is nothing the African loves so much as to sell his fellowmen. They immediately called out their names in Portuguese: one was Don Miguel, another Don Pedro, another Don Francisco. They began to jabber away in Portuguese. Where they had learned this language I could not tell, unless it were in Sangatanga. I could not understand them; so I sent my captain to talk with them. He had some difficulty to persuade them that I came no such errand as slave-trading. They insisted that I had, and that the vessel looked exactly like a slaver. They said we must buy some of their slaves; they had plenty of them.

They insisted that I should not go to Ranpano. I should put up a factory in their place. They belonged to Elindé, a town just at the mouth of the Fernand-Vaz, whose king is named Sangala. They praised the power and greatness of Sangala, and decried poor Ranpano, until I had to order all hands ashore for the night, being anxious to get a good quiet sleep to prepare for the morrow.

During the night, the men on watch said they heard the paddling of a canoe coming towards us. What could it be? Let us be ready. These men might be comingto board us and make war. At length the canoe came within hailing distance; we shouted to them. (I may say that the Commi speak the same language as the Oroungou people—the inhabitants of Cape Lopez.) They came, they said, with a message from King Sangala. I recognised the voice of the head man in the canoe to be that of Nchouga. He was brother of King Bango of Cape Lopez. Bango had accused Nchouga of bewitching him, whereupon the latter, to save his life, fled from the country; and having married one of the daughters of Sangala, he came to his father-in-law for protection.

Nchouga was a very cunning fellow; fortunately I knew him well, and he could not fool me so easily as he thought. He came to tell me that Sangala was the master of all the river; that he was a very great king; that he would not let me go to Ranpano, who was only a vassal of the great Sangala; therefore, he advised me as a friend—an old friend—to go ashore at Elindé.

I could read the cunning rogue. He had been one of the greatest rascals of Cape Lopez, and his slave dealings had not improved him. So I sent Nchouga off; I wanted to go to sleep. He had come out to test me; they thought I was a green hand at slave-trading.

Early next morning Sangala sent off a boat for me. On my arrival at Elindé, which village was about two miles from the river's mouth, I was conducted to the best house. Hither presently came King Sangala, who, in order to nerve himself for the occasion, had got drunk, and came attended by a great crowd of eager subjects. He grew very angry when I stated my intention of passing up the river, and going to Ranpano, and also into the interior. He declared that I should not go; he was the big king there and everywhere all over the world, and I must settle in his town.

I declared that I should go on. Sometimes I wonder that they did not at once make me a prisoner.

We had some sharp words, and I explained to his majesty that I was an old African traveller, and saw through all his lies; that he was not the big king of the country, as he said. Then he said I might go wherever I liked, provided I would have a factory built in his village.

I said that I had no factory to build in his village; but I offered to "dash" him (give him some presents).

He refused this offer; and now Ranpano, having just come, assured me that I should be backed up. I told Sangala I should force my way up. Sangala and all his people shouted with all their might that there should be war; Sangala, as he got up to say so, reared and tumbled down, he was so drunk.

So I left Sangala. By that time it rained so hard that no one followed us. It is wonderful how a crowd is dispersed by a shower of rain.

A great palaver was looming up; the excitement had spread over the country. In the meantime I had succeeded in going to Ranpano's village, situated up the river, five or six miles above Elindé. Ranpano gave me as much land as I wanted. My goods must come to his village; but it seemed that they could not be brought there without great trouble. Our canoes would be attacked by Sangala's people. Men would be killed; and we might be routed, unless we had a powerful force.

One morning the war drums beat. All Ranpano's friends had gathered to help fight Sangala. Canoe after canoe came in loaded with armed men, with drums beating, and all hands shouting, and waving their swords, guns, and spears. All were prepared to assist Ranpano's white man; all were anxious to burn and plunder Elindé, ready even to die in the undertaking.There was King Ritimbo, with two canoes and fifty men; King Mombon, from Sanguibiuri, also had two canoes; altogether we had no less than twenty big canoes, and could muster about three hundred men, most of whom were drunk on *mimbo* (palm-wine), and as noisy and as ready for fight as drunkenness will make an African. The drums were beaten, war songs were sung, and guns fired, as we paddled down the river. All hands had their faces painted white, which is a sign of war; and were covered with fetiches and other amulets. The white chalk or ochre was a sovereign protection against danger, and their war fetiches would prevent them from being killed. I could not recognise old Ranpano, his body was so daubed with paint.

One would have supposed these terrible fellows were bent upon the most bloody of raids. I wondered if all this uproar would end in smoke; I thought it would; nor was I disappointed. As these terrible warriors approached the village of Elindé they became less demonstrative. When they came in sight of Sangala's town, they pushed over to the other shore, out of the way, and took care to keep the Caroline between the enemy and themselves. The sight of Sangala's warriors had wrought a wonderful change in their warlike feelings. They really began to think that there might be some fighting.

We found that Sangala had also gathered his friends, and had about one hundred and fifty men ready for the fight, who probably felt about as courageous as my men did. These fellows were painted more outrageously than mine, having red as well as white applied in broad stripes. They looked like so many devils shouting and firing guns, each side knowing their mutual lack of courage, and thinking it prudent to scare the other in advance.

My men fired guns, sung, and danced war dances. I went on board my schooner. One small canoe on Sangala's side, with two men, who were unarmed, started from the shore towards us. This of course meant a palaver; they came on board of the Caroline, where I was. I sent word to Sangala, pointing to two little guns we had on deck, that if he stopped me I would blow his canoes out of the water with grape-shot, and would then go and bring a man-of-war to finish him up. I loaded my guns and pistols before them. I made my men put good charges into their pieces, and showed Sangala's men the bag of bullets I loaded them with, and then sent them back, and awaited the event.

I spied them with a glass. As soon as they landed the people surrounded them; there was a grand palaver.

Presently, from Sangala, came a small canoe to ask me ashore. Sangala sent his Konde (chief wife) to be hostage for my safety. I determined to go ashore, and, to show these negroes that I had no fear of them, I took the woman along with me, to her great joy. Ranpano and his brother kings protested against my rashness as they thought it. "Why not keep Sangala's woman on board?" said they. But I told them it was not the fashion of white people to fear anything. They looked at me as if to say, "If you are not afraid we are." All this had its effect upon them, and Ranpano and his brother kings were evidently impressed, and so also was old Sangala when he saw me come with his wife by my side.

We met on neutral ground outside his town. His army was drawn up in battle array, and made a fine savage display, many of the men wearing beautiful leopard skins about their waists. They came up to us at full trot, when we were seated, and made as thoughthey would spear us all; and, if Sangala had not been close to me, I should have thought it was to be the end of us all. Ranpano kept whispering in my ears, "Why did you not keep Sangala's wife on board?"

But this advance upon us was only a kind of military salute. Sangala, this time, had become more gentle; he was not drunk, and, thinking that perhaps there might really be a fight, he had become very quiet. He did not wish to push matters to extremity.

Presently, Sangala said he would let me pass if I would give him a barrel of rum, a big one. I refused. I said I had none. He insisted that they must rejoice and get drunk. He wanted to get drunk for several days, and drink rum to his heart's content. At last, the palaver was settled, and I gave him many presents; and thereafter King Sangala became one of my best friends.

Ranpano was delighted; he hugged Sangala; he swore eternal friendship, and said that he loved him with all his heart. Sangala returned these compliments. We made a sign, agreed upon to our men, that everything was settled. Immediately they fired guns, embarked in their canoes, and came over to Sangala's village. They made a fine display, as all their canoes came in a line, and they were singing their war songs.

They were met by Sangala's warriors; and they made a rush towards each other as if they were to have a real fight, and then all was over and they laughed over the palaver, and swore that they would not hurt each other for the world.

I need not say how glad I was that everything had ended so well. Captain Cornillo, when everything looked black, swore that he never would come again to this wild country; and the crew said I wanted them all to be murdered.

I found these Commi very good people. I tookashore canoe after canoe, loaded with goods which might well tempt these poor negroes sorely. Many of the things were brought loose to Ranpano's; and yet not a single thing was stolen, not even the value of a penny. They were proud that I had come to settle among them. I was the first white man who had done so.

I love these Commi people dearly; and I am sure they all love me also. They took such great care of me. Ranpano was a very good king, and he always tried to please me, and so did his people. Now and then they did wrong; but these poor people knew no better, and they were sorry afterwards. Not one would have tried to do me an injury, and I could sleep with my doors wide open.

CHAPTER XXII.

I BUILD A VILLAGE, AND CALL IT WASHINGTON—I START FOR THE INTERIOR—MY SPEECH ON LEAVING—THE PEOPLE APPLAUD ME VOCIFEROUSLY, AND PROMISE TO BE HONEST—WE REACH ANIAMBIA—THE "BIG KING," OLENGA-YOMBI—A ROYAL BALL IN MY HONOUR—THE SUPERSTITIONS OF THE NATIVES—A MAN TOSSED BY A BUFFALO.

I immediately began building a substantial settlement, not an *olako*. I collected from a kind of palm tree a great many leaves, with which to cover the roofs of the buildings I had to construct. I gathered also a great quantity of branches from the same palm trees, and sticks, and poles, and all that was necessary to make a house; and finally I succeeded in building quite a village, which I called Washington. My own house had five rooms; it was forty-five feet long by twenty-five wide, and cost me about fifty dollars. My kitchen, which stood by itself, cost four dollars. I had a fowl-house,containing a hundred chickens (and such nice little tiny chickens they are in that country) and a dozen ducks. My goat-house contained eighteen goats, and funny goats they were. You had to milk a dozen of them to get a pint of milk. I built a powder-house separate, for I do not like to sleep every day in a place where there is powder. I had a dozen huts for my men.

This was Washington in Africa, a very different place from Washington in America.

At the back of my village was a wide extent of prairie. In front was the river Npoulounai winding along; and I could see miles out on the way which I was soon to explore. The river banks were lined with the mangrove trees; and, looking up stream, I could at almost any time see schools of hippopotami tossing and tumbling on the flats or mud banks.

I was now ready to explore the country, and go to Aniambia, where the big king of the country lived. I bought a splendid canoe, made of large trees, which I hoped would be serviceable to me in my up-river explorations. I was now anxious to be off.

Before starting I called Ranpano and all his people together, and said that I had perfect confidence in them; that I was their white man, and had come to them through much difficulty and many dangers. (Cheers.) That Sangala's people wanted me, but I was determined to live with the honest folks of Biagano (Ranpano's village). (Tremendous applause.) That I was going away for a few days, and hoped to find my goods all safe when I came back.

At this, there were great shoutings of "You can go! Do not fear! We love you! You are our white man! We will take care of you!" and so on; amid which my sixteen men seized their paddles, and shoved off.

At nine in the evening, the moon rose; and we pulled along through what seemed a charming scene. The placid stream was shaded by the immense trees which overhung its banks; and the silence was broken, now and then, by the screech of some night-prowling blast, or, more frequently, by the sudden plunge of a playful herd of hippopotami, some of which came very dangerously near us, and might have upset our canoe.

Towards midnight, my men became very tired, and we went ashore, at a little village which was nearly deserted. We could find only three old women, who were fast asleep and were not particularly anxious to make us welcome. I was too sleepy to stand upon ceremonies, and stowed myself away under a rough shed without walls. I had scarcely lain down, when there came up, suddenly, one of those fierce tornadoes which pass over these countries in the rainy season.

Fortunately, it was a dry tornado. In my half-sleepy state I did not care to move. As the tornado had unroofed every other shed as well as mine, nothing would have been gained by moving, even if it had rained.

The next morning we paid for our lodging, not in hard cash, but with some leaves of tobacco, and up the river we paddled until we reached a village called Igala Mandé, which is situated on the banks of the river. In a two hours' walk through grass fields we found numerous birds. One, in particular, was new to me, the *Mycteria senegalensis*. It had such long legs that it fairly outwalked me. I tried to catch it; but, though it would not take to its wings, it kept so far ahead that I did not even get a fair shot at it. This *Mycteria senegalensis* is a beautiful bird, and wanders here through the grass of the prairie.

There were also great flocks of a beautiful bird, whose dark golden body-plumage and long snow-white downy necks make a very fine and marked contrast with thegreen grass. Next to these, in point of number, was the snow-white *egretta*, which is found in vast flocks all along this coast.

At last we came to Aniambia. Olenga-Yombi, the king, came in from his plantation when he heard the joyful news that a white man had arrived. I paid him a state visit. He was a drunken old wretch, surrounded by a crowd of the chief men of the town. His majesty had on a thick overcoat, but no trousers; and, early as it was, he had already taken a goodly quantity of palm-wine, and was quite drunk. I was invited to sit at his right hand.

King Olenga-Yombi was one of the ugliest fellows I ever met with. He always carried with him a long stick; and when drunk he struck at his people right and left, and shouted, "I am a big king!" Happily, they managed to keep out of his way.

At nightfall I got a guide, and went out to see if I could get a shot at something larger than a bird. We had gone but a little way, when my guide pointed out to me a couple of bright glowing spots, visible through a piece of thick brush. The fellow trembled, as he whispered "Leopard!" But I saw at once that it was only the light of a couple of fireflies which had got in proper position to make a tolerable resemblance to the glowing eyes of the dreaded leopard.

I did not think much of the bravery of my guide. What a difference between him and Aboko, Niamkala, or Fasiko! I wished that I had them with me.

At two o'clock in the morning we at last heard a grunting, which announced the approach of a herd of wild hogs. I lay in wait for them, and I was fortunate enough to kill the big boar of the pack. The rest of the herd made off without showing a desire for fight.

The next day, King Olenga-Yombi held a grand dance in my honour. All the king's wives, to the number of forty, and all the women in the town and neighbourhood were present.

Fortunately, the dance was held out in the street, and not in a room, as at Cape Lopez. The women were ranged on one side, the men opposite. At the end of the line sat the drummers, beating their huge tom-toms, which make an infernal din, enough to make one deaf; and, as if for this occasion the tom-toms were not entirely adequate, there was a series of old brass kettles, which also were furiously beaten. In addition, as if the noise was not yet enough, a number of boys sat near the drummers, and beat on hollow pieces of wood. What beauty they found in such music I cannot tell. There was of course singing and shouting; and the more loudly and energetically the horrid drums were beaten, and the worse the noise on the brass kettles, the wilder were the jumps of the male Africans, and the more disgusting the contortions of the women.

As may be imagined, to beat the tom-tom is not a labour of love; the stoutest negro is worn out in an hour; and for such a night's entertainment as this, a series of drummers was required.

The people enjoyed it vastly; their only regret was that they had not a barrel of rum in the midst of the street, with which to refresh themselves in the pauses of the dance; but they managed to get just as drunk on palm-wine, of which a great quantity was served out.

The excitement became greatest when the king danced. His majesty was pretty drunk, and his jumps were very highly applauded. His wives bowed down to his feet while he capered about, and showed towards him the deepest veneration. The drums and kettles were belaboured more furiously than ever, and the singing, or rather the shouting, became stentorian.

Of course I did not think his majesty's party pleasant enough to detain me all night. I retired, but could not sleep.

Now I think I have given you a sufficient account of a ball at Aniambia, and of how his majesty Olenga-Yombi danced.

There are two very curious fetich-houses in Aniambia, which enjoy the protection of two spirits of great power—Abambou and Mbiuri. The former is an evil spirit, a kind of devil; the latter, as far as I have been able to ascertain, is beneficent.

The little houses where these spirits sometimes condescend to come and sleep for the night were about six feet square. In the house of Abambou I saw a fire, which I was told was never permitted to go out. I saw no idol, but only a large chest, on the top of which were some white and red chalk and some red parrot-feathers. The chalk was used to mark the bodies of the devout.

Abambou is the devil of the Commi people. He is a wicked and mischievous fellow, who often lives near graves and burial-grounds, and is most comfortably lodged among the skeletons of the dead. He takes occasional walks through the country, and, if he gets angry at anyone, he has the power to cause sickness and death. The Commi people cook food for him, which is deposited in lonely places in the woods, and there they address him in a flattering manner, and ask him to be good to them, and, in consideration of their gifts, and of the great care they take of him, to let them alone. I was present once at a meeting where Abambou was being addressed in public. They cried continually: "Now we are well! Now we are satisfied! Now be our friend, Abambou, and do not hurt us!"

The offerings of plantain, bananas, sugar-cane, ground-nuts, etc., etc., are wrapped in leaves by thefree men, but the slaves lay them on the bare ground. Sometimes Abambou is entreated to kill the enemies of him who is making the offering. A bed is made in Abambou's house, and there he is believed to rest himself sometimes, when he is tired going up and down the coast in the forest.

Mbiuri, whose house I next visited, is lodged and kept much in the same way as his rival. He is a good spirit, but his powers are like those of Abambou, as far as I could make out. Not being wicked, he is less zealously worshipped.

These Commi people are full of superstition. They believe in a third and much-dreaded spirit, called Ovengua. This is a terrible catcher and *eater* of men. He is not worshipped, and has no power over disease; but he wanders unceasingly through the forests, and catches and destroys luckless travellers who cross his path. By day he lives in dark caverns, but at night he roams freely, and even sometimes gets into the body of a man, and beats and kills all who come out in the dark. Sometimes, they relate, such a spirit is met and resisted by a body of men, who wound him with spears, and even kill him. In this case the body must be burned, and not even the smallest bone left, lest a new Ovengua should arise from it. There are many places where no object in the world would induce a Commi negro to go by night, for fear of this dreadful monster.

They have a singular belief that when a person dies who has been bewitched, the bones of his body leave the grave one by one, and form in a single line united to each other, which line of bones gradually becomes an Ovengua.

It is not an easy matter to get at the religious notions of these people. They themselves have no well-defined ideas of them, and on many points they are not very communicative.

I suppose they think that sometimes the Ovengua is in a man; hence they kill him and burn his body.

Of course the Commi people, like all other negroes, are firm believers in witchcraft.

Not very far from Aniambia, there is a place in the forest which is supposed to be haunted by the spirit of a crazy woman, who, some hundreds of years ago, left her home. They believe that she cultivates her plantation in some hidden recess in the forest, and that she often lies in wait for travellers, whom she beats and kills out of pure malice.

While at Aniambia I had a great adventure with a *bos brachicheros*, which might have ended in a terrible way. I started out early one day to try and get a shot at some buffaloes which were said to be in the prairie at the back of the town. I had been an hour on the plains with Ifouta, a hunter, when we came upon a bull feeding in the midst of a little prairie surrounded by woods, which made an approach easy. I remember well how beautiful the animal looked. Ifouta walked round through the jungle opposite to where I lay in wait; for, if the animal should take fright at him, it might fly towards me. When he reached the right position, Ifouta began to crawl, in the hunter's fashion, through the grass towards his prey. All went well till he came near enough for a shot. Just then, unluckily, the bull saw him. Ifouta immediately fired. It was a long shot, and he only wounded the beast, which, quite infuriated, immediately rushed upon him. It was now that poor Ifouta lost his presence of mind. In such cases, which are continually happening to those who hunt the *bos brachicheros*, the proper course for the hunter is to remain perfectly quiet till the beast is within a jump of him, then to step nimbly to one side, and let him rush past. But Ifouta got up and ran.

The bull ran faster than he, and in a moment had him on his horns. He tossed him high into the air, once, twice, thrice, before I could come up; for, as soon as I saw what had happened, I ran as fast as I could to the rescue, and my shouts drew the bull's fury upon myself. He left Ifouta and came rushing at me, thinking that he would serve me as he had just served Ifouta. Master Bull was sadly mistaken. I took a good aim, and down came the bull, to rise no more.

Ifouta proved to be considerably bruised; but, on the whole, he was more scared than hurt. It was fortunate for him that the horns of these buffaloes slant backwards a good deal, and are curved.

CHAPTER XXIII.

CAPTURE OF A YOUNG GORILLA—I CALL HIM "FIGHTING JOE"—HIS STRENGTH AND BAD TEMPER—HE PROVES UNTAMEABLE—JOE ESCAPES—RE-CAPTURED—ESCAPES AGAIN—UNPLEASANT TO HANDLE—DEATH OF "FIGHTING JOE."

I remember well the day when I first possessed a live gorilla. Yes, a gorilla that could roar; a young gorilla alive! He was captured not far from Cape St. Catherine, and dragged into Washington.

My hunters were five in number, and were walking very silently through the forest, when suddenly the silence was broken by the cry of a young gorilla for its mother. Everything was still. It was about noon, and they immediately determined to follow the cry.

Soon they heard the cry again. Gun in hand, the brave fellows crept noiselessly towards a clump of wood where the baby gorilla evidently was. They knew the mother would be near; and there was a likelihood that they might encounter the male also, which they dread more than they do the mother. But they determined to risk everything, and, if possible, to take the young one alive, knowing how pleased I should be, for I had been long trying to capture a young gorilla.

Presently they perceived the bush moving; and crawling a little farther on, in dead silence, scarcely breathing with excitement, they beheld what had seldom been seen even by negroes. A young gorilla was seated on the ground, as the picture shows you, eating some berries, which grew close to the earth. A few feet farther on sat the mother, also eating of the same fruit.

Instantly they made ready to fire; and none too soon, for the old female saw them as they raised their guns, and they had to pull triggers without delay. Happily, they wounded her mortally.

She fell on her face, the blood gushing from the wounds. The young one, hearing the noise of the guns, ran to his mother and clung to her, hiding his face and embracing her body. The hunters immediately rushed towards the two, hallooing with joy. How much I wished that I had been with them, and been so fortunate as to assist in the capture of a live gorilla!

Their shouts roused the little one, who, by this time, was covered with blood coming from his mother'swounds. He instantly let go of his mother and ran to a small tree, which he climbed with great agility. There he sat and roared at them savagely. They were now perplexed how to get at him.

What was to be done? No one cared to run the chance of being bitten by this savage little beast. They did not want to shoot him, for they knew I should never forgive them for doing so. He would not come down the tree, and they did not care to climb it after him. At last they cut down the tree, and, as it fell, they dexterously threw a cloth over the head of the young monster, and thus gained time to secure it while it was blinded. With all these precautions, one of the men received a severe bite on the hand, and another had a piece taken out of his leg.

The little brute, though very diminutive, and the merest baby in age, was astonishingly strong, and by no means good-tempered. They found they could not lead him. He constantly rushed at them, showing fight, and manifesting a strong desire to take a piece, or several pieces, out of every one of their legs, which were his special objects of attack. So they were obliged to get a forked stick, in which his neck was inserted in such a way that he could not escape, and yet could be kept at a safe distance. It must have been very uncomfortable for him; but it was the only way of securing themselves against his nails and teeth, and thus he was brought to Washington.

The excitement in the village was intense, as the animal was lifted out of the canoe in which he had come down the river. He roared and bellowed; and looked around wildly with his wicked little eyes, giving fair warning that if he could get at any of us he would take his revenge. Of course, no one came in his way.

I saw that the stick hurt his neck, and immediately set about having a cage made for him. In two hours we had built a strong bamboo house with the slats securely tied at such a distance apart that we could see the gorilla, and it could see out. We made it as strong as we could, and I was very careful to provide against every chance of his escaping. In this cage he was immediately deposited; and now, for the first time, I had a fair chance to look at my prize.

As I approached the cage he darted at me; but I could afford to have a good laugh over him, for I knew he could not get near enough to bite me. He looked at me with very savage eyes.

I named the gorilla Joe—"Fighting Joe." He was evidently not three years old, but fully able to walk alone, and possessed, for his age, of very extraordinary strength. His height was about three feet and six inches. His hands and face were very black, his eyes were sunken. The hair on his head was of a reddish-brown colour. It began just at the eyebrows and came down the sides of the face to the lower jaw, just as our beards grow. The whiskers, if we may call them so, were of a blackish colour. The face was smooth, and intensely black. The upper lip was covered with short, coarse hair; I wondered if it was the beginning of a moustache. I found afterwards that gorillas had no moustaches. The lower lip had longer hair; and I wondered also if in time an imperial would grow there. There were eyelashes too, though these were slight and thin. The eyebrows were straight. Excepting the face, and the palms of his hands and feet, his whole body was covered with hair. On the back, the hair was of an iron grey, becoming quite dark near the arms. On the arms, the hair was longer than anywhere else on the body, as you may see by the picture.

After I had looked carefully at the little fellow, andknew well that he was safely locked in his cage, I ventured to approach him to say a few encouraging words. He stood in the farthest corner; but as I approached, he bellowed and made a precipitate rush at me. Though I retreated as quickly as I could, he succeeded in catching my trousers' legs with the toes of one of his feet, and then retreated immediately to the farthest corner. This taught me caution; I must not approach too near.

Shall I be able to tame him? I thought I should; but I was disappointed.

He sat in his corner, looking wickedly out of his grey eyes; and I never saw a more morose or ill-tempered face than this little beast had. I do not believe that gorillas ever smile.

Of course I had to attend to the wants of my captive. My first business in the morning was to attend on Joe. I sent for some of the forest berries which these animals are known to prefer, and placed these and a cup of water within his reach. He was exceedingly shy, and would neither eat nor drink till I had removed to a considerable distance.

The second day I found Joe fiercer than on the first. He rushed savagely at anyone who stood even for a moment near his cage and seemed ready to tear us to pieces. A fine specimen of man-monkey, thought I; a tiger under the disguise of a gorilla. I wondered what kind of a cage a full-grown gorilla would require. I should certainly not care to be his keeper.

I threw Joe pieces of pine-apple leaves; and I noticed that he ate only the white part. There seemed to be no difficulty about his food, as long as it was gathered from his native woods; but he refused all other kinds of food. He was very fond of bananas and ripe plantains.

The third day Joe was still more morose and savage, bellowing when any persons approached, or retiring to a distant corner to make a rush upon them.

On the fourth day, while no one was near, the little rascal succeeded in forcing apart two of the bamboo sticks which composed his cage and made his escape. I came up just as his flight was discovered, and immediately got all the negroes together for pursuit. Where had he gone? I was determined to surround the wood and recapture him. Running into my house to get one of my guns, I was startled by an angry growl issuing from under my low bedstead. It was Master Joe; there was no mistake about it; I knew his growl but too well. Master Joe lay there hid, but anxiously watching my movements. I cleared out faster than I came in. I instantly shut the windows, and called to my people to guard the door. When Joe saw the crowd of black faces he became furious; and with his eyes glaring, and every sign of rage in his little face and body, he got out from beneath the bed. He was about to make a rush at all of us. He was not afraid. A stampede of my men took place. I shut the door quickly, and left Joe master of the premises. I preferred devising some plans for his easy capture, to exposing myself and men to his terrible teeth; for the little rascal could bite very hard, and I did not care to have a piece taken out of one of my legs. How to take him was now a puzzling question. He had shown such strength and such rage already that I did not care, and none of my men seemed to care, to run the chance of getting badly beaten in a hand-to-hand struggle, in which we were pretty sure to come off the worse. Meantime, peeping through the keyhole, I saw Master Joe standing still in the middle of the room looking about for his enemies, and examining, with some surprise, the furniture. He seemed to think that he had never seen such things before. I watched withfear, lest the ticking of my clock should attract his attention, and perhaps lead him to an assault upon that precious article. Indeed, I should have left Joe in possession, but for a fear that he would destroy the many little articles of value or curiosity I had hung about the walls, and which reminded me so much of America.

Finally, seeing Joe to be quiet, I despatched some fellows for a net; and, opening the door quickly, I threw this over his head. Fortunately we succeeded at the first throw in effectually entangling the young monster, who roared frightfully, and struck and kicked in every direction under the net. So fearfully was he excited that I thought he would die in a fit of rage. I took hold of the back of his neck; two men seized his arms, and another the legs; and, thus held by four men, we could hardly manage Joe.

We carried him as quickly as we could to the cage, which had been repaired, and then once more locked him in. I never saw such a furious beast in my life as he was. He darted at everyone. He bit the bamboos of his cage. He glared at us with venomous and sullen eyes, and in every motion showed a temper thoroughly wicked and malicious.

After this Joe got worse than ever; and as good treatment only made him more morose and savage, I tried what starvation would do towards breaking his spirit. Besides, it began to be troublesome to procure his food from the woods, and I wanted him to become accustomed to civilized food, which was placed before him. But he would touch nothing of the kind. How was I to bring him to America? I could not put an African forest on board. As for his temper, after starving him for twenty-four hours, all I gained was, that he came slowly up and took some berries from the forest out of my hand and then immediately retreatedto his corner to eat them. Daily attentions from me, for a fortnight more, did not bring me any further confidence from him than this. He always snarled at me; and only when very hungry would he take even his choicest food from my hand.

At the end of this fortnight I came one day to feed him, and found that he had gnawed a bamboo to pieces slily, and again made his escape. Luckily he had but just gone, for as I looked around I caught a sight of him making off on all fours, and with great speed, across the prairie for a clump of trees.

I at once gave the alarm. I called the men up, and we gave chase, taking with us all the fishing nets. He saw us, and, before we could head him off, made for another clump, which was thicker and larger. This we surrounded. He did not ascend a tree, but stood defiantly at the border of the wood. About one hundred and fifty of us surrounded him. As we moved up he began to yell, and made a sudden dash upon a poor fellow who was in advance. The fellow ran, and tumbled down in affright. By his fall he escaped the tender mercies of Joe's teeth; but he also detained the little rascal long enough for the nets to be thrown over him.

Four of us bore him again, struggling, into the village. This time I would not trust him to the cage, but fastened a small chain round his neck. This operation he resisted with all his might, and it took us quite an hour to securely chain the little fellow, whose strength was something marvellous.

Ten days after he was thus chained he died quite suddenly. He had been in good health, and ate plentifully of his natural food, which was brought every day from the forest for him. He did not seem to sicken until two days before his death. He died in some pain. To the last he continued utterly untameable, and after his chain was put on he added treachery to his other vices. He would come sometimes quite readily to eat out of my hand, but while I stood by him would suddenly—looking me all the time in the face to keep my attention—put out his foot and grasp at my leg. Several times he tore my pantaloons in this manner. A quick retreat on my part saved my legs from further injury, but I had to be very careful in my approaches. The negroes could not come near him at all without setting him in a rage. He seemed always to remember that they captured him, and to think he had experienced rather too hard treatment at their hands; but he evidently always cherished towards me also a feeling of revenge.

After he was chained I filled a half barrel with hay, and set it near him for his bed. He recognised its use at once, and it was pretty to see him shake up the hay and creep into this nest when he was tired. At night he always shook it up, and then took some hay in his hands, with which he would cover himself when he was snug in his barrel. He often moaned, for his mother perhaps, at night.

After Joe died I stuffed his body, and brought his skin and skeleton to New York, where many saw it. Around his neck, where the chain had been, the hair was worn off.

Poor Joe! I wish he had lived and become tame, so that I could have brought him home with me to show the children.

Now poor Joe can be seen stuffed in the British Museum.

CHAPTER XXIV.

THE HIPPOPOTAMUS—A DUEL—SHOOTING ON THE RIVER—
NEARLY UPSET—A NIGHT-HUNT ON LAND—MY COMPANION
FIRES AND RUNS—APPEARANCE AND HABITS OF THE
HIPPOPOTAMUS.

What have we yonder in the water? A flock of hippopotami! Their bodies look for all the world like so many old weather-beaten logs stranded on a mud-bank or a sand-bar.

Every thing was still. The sun was very hot, and all nature seemed to repose. I was concealed on thebanks of the river, under a very shady tree, watching them. Suddenly, not far from me, two huge beasts rose as by enchantment to the surface of the water and rushed towards each other. Their vast and hideous mouths were opened to their utmost capacity, showing their huge crooked tusks, which gave their mouths a savage appearance. Their eyes were flaming with rage, and each of them put forth all his power to annihilate the other. They seized each other with their jaws; they stabbed and punched with their strong tusks, lacerating each other in a frightful manner; they advanced and retreated; now they were at the top of the water, and now they sank down to the bottom. Their blood discoloured the river, and their groans or grunts of rage were hideous to listen to. They showed little power of strategy, but rather a piggish obstinacy in maintaining their ground, and a frightful savageness of demeanour. The combat lasted an hour. It was a grand sight. The water around them was sometimes white with foam. At last one turned about and made off, leaving the other victorious and master of the field. A few days after, I killed a hippopotamus, and its thick hide was lacerated terribly. Doubtless it was one of the beasts I had seen fighting.

The hippopotamus is found in most of the rivers of Africa which empty themselves into the Atlantic or Indian Ocean, but in none but the Nile of those which empty themselves into the Mediterranean; and in the Nile it is only met far up the river. Many as there were of them on the Fernand-Vaz, they were more numerous on the Ogobai.

How much sport I have had with them! How often have I studied their habits! And now I must give you some account of my encounters with them.

About five miles above my little settlement at Washington there was a place in the river shallowenough for them to stand and play around, and there they remained all day playing in the deep water, sometimes diving, but for the most part standing on the shallows, with only their ugly noses or heads lifted out of the water.

One fine morning I went towards them. We approached slowly and with caution to within thirty yards of them without seeming to attract the slightest attention from the sluggish animals. One might have asked himself, "Are they hippopotami or not?" Stopping there I fired five shots, and, so far as I could see, I killed three hippopotami. The ear is one of the most vulnerable spots, and this was my mark every time.

The first shot was received with very little attention by the herd; but the struggles of the dying animal I had hit, which turned over several times and finally sank to the bottom, seemed to rouse the others, who began to plunge about and dive down into deep water. The blood of my victims discoloured the water all around, and we could not see whether those who escaped were not swimming for us.

Presently the canoe received a violent jar, and, looking overboard, we perceived that we were in the midst of the herd. "The hippopotami are coming upon us!" shouted the men; "they are going to attack us!" We pulled out of the way as fast as we could, none of us being anxious to be capsized. It would have been a comical sight to see us swimming in the midst of a flock of hippopotami, and some of us, perhaps, raised up on the back of one as he came to the surface, or lifted, maybe, with his two crooked tusks in our body.

We were soon out of the way, and looking back to see where were the animals I had killed, I saw nothing. They had sunk to the bottom, and of thethree, only one was recovered. It was found two days afterwards on a little island near the river's mouth. Seeing this, I resolved never to shoot hippopotami while they are in the water, for I did not want to kill these animals for nothing; I wanted their skins and their skeletons to enrich our museums.

Some time after Joe had died, I determined to go on a night hunt after hippopotami. These animals come ashore by night to feed.

The Fernand-Vaz runs for many miles parallel with the seashore, separated from the sea by a strip of sandy prairie. On this prairie the hippopotamus feeds. He is sometimes called the sea-horse, for when his head is out of the water it looks from a distance exactly like the head of a horse. The "walk" of a herd is easily discernible. It looks very much like a regular beaten road, only their immense footprints showing who are its makers. In their track no grass grows. They always return by the same path they go out on. This gives the hunter a great advantage.

I chose moonlight night, and paddled up to the vicinity of one of these "walks." There Igala, my hunter, and I set out by ourselves. I had painted my face with a mixture of oil and soot, which is a prudent measure for a white hunter in Africa. The beasts there seem to have a singularly quick eye for anything white. I made myself look exactly like Igala. We both had black faces and black hands. I was dressed in the usual dark suit of clothes for the night; people there must not go hunting in light-coloured garments. We chose the windward side of the track, for the hippopotamus has a very keen scent, and is easily alarmed at night, feeling, probably, that on land his sluggish movements, huge bulk, and short legs have their disadvantages.

We lay down under shelter of a bush and watched. As yet none of the animals had come out of the water. We could hear them in the distance splashing about in the water, their subdued snort-like roars breaking in upon the stillness of the night in a very odd way. It was the only noise we heard—no, I cannot say the only noise, for the mosquitoes were busily buzzing around, and feeding upon us, taking advantage, apparently, of our anxiety to keep perfectly quiet.

The moon was nearly down, and the watch was getting tedious, when I was startled by a sudden groan. Peering into the distance, I saw dimly a huge animal looking doubly monstrous in the uncertain light. It was quietly eating grass, which it seemed to nibble off quite close to the ground.

There was another bush between us and our prey, and we crawled up to this in dead silence. Arrived there, we were but eight yards from the great beast. How terrible he looked! The negroes who hunt the hippopotami are sometimes killed; I thought that one of us might be killed also. The animal, if only wounded, turns savagely upon his assailants, and experience has taught the negro hunters that the only safe way to approach him is from behind. He cannot turn quickly, and thus the hunter has a chance to make good his escape. This time we could not get into a very favourable position; but I determined to have my shot nevertheless, eight yards being a safe killing distance, even with so poor a light as we had by this time.

We watched the hippopotamus intently, looking at each other as if to say, "Are you ready?" We then raised our guns slowly. Igala and I both took aim. He fired and, without waiting to see the result, ran as swiftly as a good pair of legs could carry him. I was not quite ready, but fired the moment after him, and before I could get ready for running (in which I hadnot Igala's practice) I saw there was no need for it. The beast tottered for a moment, and fell over with a booming sound, dead.

This closed our night's sport, as none of the herd would come this way while their companion lay there. So we returned home. Poor Igala remonstrated with me for not running as he did. It appears that running was considered one of the chief accomplishments of the hippopotamus hunter. Our good luck created great joy in the village, where meat was scarce. The men went out at daylight and brought the flesh home. Basket after basket came in, and as each one arrived all shouted except those who did not eat the hippopotamus. It is *roonda* for them. Some of their ancestry had a long time ago given birth to a hippopotamus, and if they were to eat any, more births of hippopotami would come to them, or they would die. These shouted, "I wish he had killed a bullock instead of a hippopotamus."

The meat does not taste unlike beef, but was not so red. It was rather coarse-grained, and in the case of this animal it was not fat. It makes a welcome and wholesome dish. I tried to have some steaks; I must say they were rather tough, and did not go down easily. The broth was better, and I enjoyed it very much. There was something novel in having hippopotamus soup.

I have killed a good many hippopotami. It is a very clumsily-built, unwieldy animal, remarkable chiefly for its enormous head, whose upper jaw seemed to be movable, like the crocodile's, and for its disproportionately short legs. The male is much larger than the female; indeed, a full-grown male sometimes attains the bulk, though not the height, of the elephant. In the larger specimens the belly almost sweeps the ground as they walk.

The feet are curiously constructed to facilitate walking among the reeds and mud of the river bottom, and swimming with ease. The hoof is divided into four short, apparently clumsy and unconnected toes; and they are able, by this breadth of foot, to walk rapidly even through the mud. I have seen them make quick progress, when alarmed, in water so deep that their backs were just at the surface.

The colour of the skin is a clayey yellow, assuming a roseate hue under the belly. In the grown animal the colour is a little darker. The skin of an adult hippopotamus is from one and a half to two inches thick on the middle of the back. It is devoid of hair, with the exception of a few short bristly hairs in the tail, and a few scattered tufts, of four or five hairs each, near the muzzle.

All along the Fernand-Vaz there were scattered herds of hippopotami; and I used to watch them from my house. I could see them at any time during the day. After they have chosen a spot, they like to remain there day after day, and month after month, unless they are disturbed, or their food becomes scarce. These animals consort together in herds of from two to thirty. They choose shallows in the rivers, where the depth of the water allows them to have their whole body submerged when standing. There they remain all day, swimming off into the deep place, diving for their grassy food, or gambolling in the waves. From time to time they throw up a stream of water two or three feet high. This is done with a noise like blowing, and it is doubtless an effort to get breath. It is pleasant to watch a herd peacefully enjoying themselves, particularly when they have two or three young ones among them. Some of the little fellows look very small, and are comically awkward. They chase each other about the shoals or play about theirdams; and I have often seen them seated on the back of their mother in the water. How careful their mothers seemed to be when they were swimming about, and carrying their young in the way I have described. It is a sight worth seeing; sometimes the whole herd of hippopotami will disappear for a long time under the water.

They prefer parts of the rivers where the current is not very swift, and are therefore to be found in all the lakes of the interior. They prefer to be near grass fields. They are very fond of a particular kind of coarse grass which grows on these prairies, and will travel considerable distances to find it. They always return, however, before daylight. Their path overland is very direct. Neither rocks nor swamps nor bushes can prove formidable obstacles to a water beast of such bulk. I have seen their path lie through the thickest woods. Unless much pursued and harassed, they are not much afraid of man. If troubled by hunters they move their encampment, or go into countries where they can be more quiet.

Some of their favourite grass was growing on a little plain at the back of my house; and several times I found hippopotami tracks not more than fifty yards from the house. They had not feared to come as near as this; though probably, if the wind had been blowing towards them, they would have avoided the place.

They always choose a convenient landing-place, where the bank has a long and easy incline. This landing-place they use till they have eaten up all the provender which can be found in that vicinity. Before going ashore, they watch for an hour, and sometimes for two hours, near the landing, remaining very quiet themselves, and listening for danger. The slightest token of the hunter's presence, or any other suspicious appearances on such occasions, will send them away for that night. If no danger appears they begin to wander ashore in twos or threes. I never saw more than three of a herd grazing together; and, during their stay ashore, they place more dependence on their ears than on their eyes. I have watched them closely in many hunts; and I am sure that the beast walks along with his eyes nearly shut.

When playing in the water, this animal makes a noise very much resembling the grunt of a pig. This grunt it utters also when alarmed by the approach of man. When enraged, or suddenly disturbed, it utters a kind of groan—a hoarse sound—which can be heard at a considerable distance. They are quite combative among themselves, as you have seen in the case of the fight I have described.

CHAPTER XXV.

VISIT OF KING QUENGUEZA—I PROMISE TO VISIT HIM—THE KINDNESS OF THE COMMI—THE DRY SEASON ON THE FERNAND-VAZ—PLENTY OF BIRDS AND FISHES—THE MARABOUTS—THE EAGLES—A BAD WOUND.

One fine day I was quietly seated in my bamboo house, and reading over, for the fiftieth time, the letters of the dear friends who had not forgotten me, and were so kind as to remember me in my wandering life in Africa. My attention was suddenly drawn away by the singing of numerous voices coming down the river. Soon afterwards there stood before me, accompanied by Ranpano, a tall venerable-looking and slender negro of noble but savage bearing; he was evidently, I thought, a chief; there was something commanding about his countenance. He was not very dark. The people who came with him showed him great respect. This tall negro was Quengueza, the great king of the Rembo, and the sovereignof the whole up-river country of the Rembo and Ovenga, the head waters of the Fernand-Vaz.

He came down in considerable state in three canoes, with three of his favourite wives, and about one hundred and thirty men.

My little black boy, Macondai, brought him a chair; and after he had seated himself I saluted him, according to the usual custom, by saying "Mbolo." After a few seconds he said "Ai." Then he paused a little while, and said "Mbolo," to which I replied "Ai." This is the usual mode of salutation in the Commi country, the host beginning first.

He looked at me and seemed very much astonished. He said he expected to see a tall and stout man. He had heard of me as a great hunter. He was now convinced, he said, that I must have a brave heart to hunt as I did.

Fortunately, Quengueza and I could talk together, the Commi being his native language.

He told me there were plenty of gorillas and *nshiegos* in his country; and that, if I would come, I should have liberty and protection to hunt and to do what I pleased. No one would hurt my people, or Ranpano's people, or myself, or anybody, added he, with emphasis, that should come with me.

I liked the old king at first sight; but I little guessed then that he would afterwards become so fond of me, and that I should love him so much. Yes, I shall remember my good friend Quengueza as long as I live. Though he is a poor heathen, his heart was full of love for me, and he possessed many manly and noble qualities.

I was so much pleased with King Quengueza's visit that I sent the kind-hearted old fellow off with his canoes full of presents of iron bars, brass rods, chests, etc.; and I gave him goods on trust with which to buyme ebony. He promised me great sport, and an introduction to some tribes of whom these Commi men of the seashore knew nothing.

To do him greater honour my people fired a salute as he started off, with which he was highly delighted, as an African is sure to be with noise. He did not go before making me promise to come and see him as soon as the rainy season arrived.

The dry season was now setting in. It was the first I had spent in the Commi country; and I devoted the whole month of July to exploring the country along the seashore, between the Fernand-Vaz and the sea.

There was quite a change. The birds, which were so abundant during the rainy season, had taken their leave; and other birds, in immense numbers, flocked in to feed on the fish, which now leave the seashore and the bars of the river's mouth and ascend the river to spawn. Fish, particularly mullet, were so abundant in the river that two or three times, when I took my evening airing on the water in a flat upper-river canoe, enough mullet would leap into the boat to furnish me a breakfast the next day. The quantity of fish in the shallow water was prodigious.

The breakers on the shore, never very light, were now frightful to see. The coast was rendered inaccessible by them even to the natives, and the surf increased to such a degree, even at the mouth of the river, that it was difficult, and often impossible, to enter with a canoe. Strong winds from the south prevailed, and, though the sky was constantly overcast, not a drop of rain fell. The thermometer fell sometimes early in the morning to 64° of Fahrenheit, and I suffered from cold, as did also the poor natives. The grass on the prairie was dried up or burnt over; the ponds were dried up; only the woods kept their resplendent green.

I was often left alone in that great prairie with my cook and my little boy Macondai, and a dear little boy he was. I felt perfectly safe among the good Commi. I always had tried to do right with them, and I had reaped my reward. They loved me, and anyone who should have tried to injure me would have no doubt been put to death or exiled from the country. I shall always remember my little village of Washington and the good Commi people. When perchance I got a chill the whole village was in distress. No one was allowed to talk loud, and everyone would call during the day and sit by me with a sad face for hours without saying a word, and, when they went away, they all expressed their sorrow to see me ill. The kind women would bring me wild fruits, or cold water from the spring, in which to bathe my burning and aching head; and sometimes tears would drop from their eyes and run down their kind black faces.

At this season the negroes leave their villages and work on their plantations. The women gathered the crop of ground-nuts which had been planted the preceding rainy season, while the men cut down the trees for the plantations of the coming year, or built canoes, or idled about or went fishing. Some of their farms are necessarily at some distance off. The sandy prairie is not fit to cultivate, being, in fact, only a deposit of the sea, which must have taken an incalculable period of time to form.

The birds flocked in immense numbers on the prairies, whither they come to hatch their young; especially later in the season, when the ugly marabouts, from whose tails our ladies get the splendid feathers for their bonnets, were there in thousands; and I can assure you they were not very easy to approach. I believe the marabout is the ugliest bird I ever saw, and one would never dream that their beautifulfeathers are found only under the tail, and can hardly be seen when the bird is alive.

Pelicans waded on the river banks all day in prodigious swarms, and gulped down the luckless fish which came in their way. I loved to see them swimming about in grave silence, and every now and then grabbing up a poor fish with their enormous, long, and powerful bills. If not hungry, they left the fish in their huge pouches, till sometimes three or four pounds of reserved food awaited the coming of their appetite. This pouch, you see, performed the office of a pocket, where boys, when not hungry, keep their apples in reserve.

On the sandy islands were seen now and then flocks of the *Ibis religiosa*, the sacred Ibis of the Egyptians. They looked exactly like those that are found mummified, and which have been preserved several thousand years. They are very curious-looking birds; the head and neck have no feathers. I have tried to find their nests, but never succeeded.

Ducks of various kinds built their nests in every creek and on every new islet that appeared with the receding waters. Some of them were of beautiful plumage.

Cranes, too, and numerous other water-fowls, flocked in, and every day brought with it new birds. They came by some strange instinct, from far-distant lands, to feed upon the vast shoals of fish which literally filled the river. I wondered if many of these birds had come from the Nile, the Niger, the Zambesi—from the interior of Africa, where no one had ever penetrated, and from the vast plains of South Africa. What great travellers some of these birds must be! I envied them, and often wished I could fly away, supported by their wings. What countries I should have seen!—what curious people I should have looked at!—and how many novel things I should have found to recount to you!

Along the trees bordering the river, sometimes perched on their highest branches, sometimes hidden in the midst of them, I could see that most beautiful eagle, the *Gypohierax angolensis*, called *coungou* by the natives. This eagle is of a white and black colour. He often watches over the water. How quickly his keen eyes can see through it! and with what rapidity he darts at his prey! Then, seizing it in his powerful talons, which sink deep into it, he rises into the air and goes where he can devour it undisturbed. These eagles attack large fish. They generally make them blind, and then gradually succeed in getting them ashore, though it is hard work for them. They have a luxurious time on the Fernand-Vaz river during the dry season, and are very numerous. They build their nests on the tops of the highest trees, and come back to them every year. These nests are exactly like those you have seen, only larger. They keep very busy when their young begin to eat. The male and female are then continually fishing. Strange to say, they are very fond of the palm-oil nuts. In the season, when these are ripe, they are continually seen among the palm trees.

No wonder these eagles grab fish so easily, they have such claws! One day, as one passed over my head, I shot him, and, thinking that he was quite dead, I took him up, when suddenly, in the last struggle for life, his talons got into my hands. I could have dropped down from pain. Nothing could have taken the claws away; one of them went clear through my hand, and I shall probably keep the mark of it all my life.

On the seashore I sometimes caught a bird called the *Sula capensis*, which had been driven ashore bythe treacherous waves to which it had trusted itself, and could not, for some mysterious reason, get away again.

Finally, every sand-bar was covered with gulls, whose shrill screams were heard from morning till night, as they flew about greedily after their finny prey.

It was a splendid opportunity for sportsmen, and I thought of some of my friends. As for myself, I took more delight in studying the habits of the birds than in killing them, and I assure you I had a very delightful time. I love dearly the dry season in Africa. I am sure you would have enjoyed it quite as much as I did, if you had been there with me.

CHAPTER XXVI.

ANOTHER EXPEDITION TO LAKE ANENGUE—DIFFICULT PASSAGE UP THE RIVER—THE CROCODILES—KING DAMAGONDAI AND HIS TROUBLES—I BUY AN MBUITI, OR IDOL.

One fine morning there was a great bustle on the banks of the river at Washington, where two canoes were loading. I was about to start on another expedition. I called King Ranpano and his people together and gave them charge of my property; I declared that if anything was stolen during my absence I should surely punish the thief.

They all protested that I need not even lock the doors of my house; and I believed them. The Biagano people loved me, and did not steal from me.

Then I counted my ten goats in their presence, and said that I wanted no leopard stories told me when I came back. At this they shouted and laughed. They declared that neither they nor the leopards should touch my goats.

I counted the fowls, and told them I wanted no snake stories about them. Another hearty laugh, and they all shouted that no snakes should gobble up my fowls. These matters having been satisfactorily arranged, I started with my canoes and a well-armed crew.

I was bound again for Lake Anengue, where I had been a few months before. It was now the dry season. We had armed ourselves well, for fear we might be interrupted, as some people came up this way to make plantations during the dry season and might dispute our advance; I determined to let no man bar the road to me.

The dry season was at its height, and I found the Npoulounay shallower than before. There was about fifteen feet less depth of water in the Ogobai during the dry season than there was in the rainy season. At this time the river was covered with muddy or sandy islands, many of which were left dry. The muddy islands were covered with reeds, among which sported the flamingo, a bird not seen here in the rainy season.

We pulled hard all day, and we slept the first night on a sandy island of the Ogobai river, under our mosquito-nets, of which I had laid in a store. These nets, which the natives also use, are made of grass cloth, which comes from the far interior, and does very well out doors, where it keeps out the dew as well as the mosquitoes, and protects the sleeper against the cold winds which prevail.

The next morning, when I awoke, I saw, for the first time, a fog in this part of Africa; it was very thick, but the sun drove it off. I sent out my fishing-net, and in a few minutes the men caught fish enough for supper and breakfast.

After our breakfast of fish and plantain, we paddled on up the stream. Though we had seen a few villages, we had not met a single canoe on the water, and nothing human, except a corpse that came down the river and ran against our canoe. It was probably the body of some poor wretch who had been drowned on account of witchcraft. The hands and feet were tied, so that when they threw him into the water he could not swim.

Finally we entered the Anengue; but this river we found was entirely changed since May. Then it was a deep, swift stream. Now its surface was dotted with numberless black mud islands, on which swarmed incredible numbers of crocodiles. We actually saw many hundreds of these disgusting monsters, sunning themselves on the black mud, and slipping off into the water to feed. I never saw such a horrible sight. Many were at least twenty feet long; and when they opened their frightful mouths they seemed capable of swallowing our little canoes without trouble. I wondered what would become of us all if, perchance, our canoe should capsize.

I determined to have a shot at these crocodiles, which seemed no wise frightened at our approach. Making my men paddle the boat quite near to them, I singled out the biggest and lodged a ball in his body, aiming at the joints of his fore legs, where the thick armour is defective. He tumbled over, and, after struggling in the water for a moment, sank into the mud. His companions turned their hideous snaky eyes down at him, in momentary surprise, but did notknow what to make of it, and dropped back to their sluggish comfort. I shot another, but he sank also, and as my men did not like to venture into the black mud after them, we got neither.

As we ascended the stream, it branched off in several places, and became gradually narrower. Crocodiles were seen everywhere. At length we found ourselves pushing laboriously along through a deep crooked ditch, not more than two yards wide, and overhung with tall reeds, on which a great number of birds balanced themselves, as though enjoying our dilemma. We found this time, to my surprise, a tremendous current running. In May, the water of the lake had overflowed its shores, and its regular outlets had therefore no great pressure upon them. Now, this outlet was choked with water, which rushed through at such a rate that at some of the turns in the crooked channel we were actually swept back several times before we could make our way ahead. At one point, where the true outlets joined, we could not pass till I made the men smoke their *condouquai*, a long reed pipe, which seems to give them new vigour; I also gave them a sup of my brandy. This done, they gave a great shout and pushed through, and in an hour after we emerged into the lake, but not without tremendous exertions.

We now lay on our paddles and gazed about us. On one side the lake is bounded by hills which come close down to the shore; on the other side the hills recede, and between them and the water lies a dreary extent of low marsh, covered with reeds. Several towns were in sight, all located on the summits of hills.

The lake, alas! had changed with the season too. It was still a beautiful sheet of water; but all over its placid face the dry season had brought out an eruption of those black mud islands which we had noticed before, and on these reposed, I fear to say what number ofcrocodiles. Wherever the eye was turned these disgusting creatures, with their dull leering eyes and huge savage jaws, appeared in prodigious numbers. The water was alive with fish, on which I suppose the crocodiles had fat living; but pelicans and herons, ducks and other water-birds, also abounded, drawn hither by the abundance of their prey.

Paddling carefully past great numbers of crocodiles, into whose ready jaws I was by no means anxious to fall, and past several villages, whose people looked at us with mute amazement, we reached at last the town of Damagondai. A great crowd was assembled to receive us, headed by the king himself, who stood on the shore. Quarters were provided for me by his majesty, who, a short time after my arrival, presented me with a goat. He was dressed in the usual middle-cloth of the natives, and a tarnished scarlet soldier's coat, but was innocent of trousers. His welcome, however, was not the less hearty because the pantaloons were absent.

His town, which contains about fifty huts, lies on some high ground, at a little distance from the water. I distributed presents among the grey-beards, and beads among the women, and thus put them all in good humour.

Damagondai, the king, then insisted that I must get married to at least two or three women. He was amazed when I declined this flattering proposal, and insisted upon it that my bachelor life must be very lonely and disagreeable.

The king was a tall, rather slim negro, over six feet high, and well-shaped. In war, or in the chase, he had the usual amount of courage, but at home he was exceedingly superstitious. As night came on he seemed to get a dread of death; and at last began to groan that some of the people wanted to bewitch him, in order to get his property and his authority. Finallyhe would get excited, and begin to curse all witches and sorcerers. He would say that no one should have his wives and slaves; and that the people who wanted to kill him had better beware; the *mboundou* was ready.

Certainly poor Damagondai must have slept on the wrong side, as I told him afterwards, for the old fellow began to lecture his wives, telling them to love him and feed him well, for he had given a great deal of goods and slaves to their parents for them, and they were a constant expense to him. To all this the poor women listened with respect.

Damagondai and I were very good friends. I really don't know why, but, wherever I went, these negroes seem to take a liking to me.

In the village of Damagondai there was an *mbuiti*, "an idol," representing a female figure, with copper eyes, and a tongue made of a sharp sword-shaped piece of iron. This explained her chief attribute; she cuts to pieces those with whom she is displeased. She was dressed in the Shekiani cloth, covering her from the neck down. She is said to speak, to walk, to foretell events, and to take vengeance on her enemies. Her house is the most prominent one in the whole village.

She comes to people by night and tells them in their sleep what is going to happen. In this way, they asserted, my coming had been foretold. They worship her by dancing around her and singing her praises, and their requests. Sometimes a single woman or man comes alone to prefer a request; and one evening I saw the whole village engaged in this rite, all dancing and singing around her. They offer her sugar-cane and other food, which they believe she eats. I tried to buy this goddess, but, ugly as she was, Damagondai said that no amount of money would purchase her. He insinuated, however, in a very slight way, that for aproper price I might obtain the mbuiti of the slaves. Then a great council took place with the grey-beards of the village. The slaves were on the plantations. They agreed to tell them on their return that they had seen their mbuiti walk off in the woods, and that she had not returned. I could hear them laugh over what they thought to be their clever plot.

I paid them a good price for it. I packed the mbuiti up, and took her off with me, and her portrait, an exact likeness, taken in New York from the idol itself, is found in my book called "Equatorial Africa."

I have often thought since how much I should have enjoyed seeing the return of the slaves to the village. I should like to know if they really believed that their mbuiti had left them; if so, there must have been great wailing and mourning for fear that the wrath of the mbuiti would come upon them.

CHAPTER XXVII.

A VISIT TO KING SHIMBOUVENEGANI—HIS ROYAL COSTUME—HUNTING CROCODILES—HOW THEY SEIZE THEIR PREY—THE NKAGO—THE OGATA.

I resolved to embark again on the waters of the Anengue Lake and make a little journey of exploration. Damagondai went in the canoe with me. He was to take me to another king, a friend of his.

We reached the residence of King Shimbouvenegani, a king with a long name and a small village. Wehad to paddle through very shallow water before reaching this place.

When we arrived, the king with the long name was not at his village. We were told he was at his *olako*—a place temporarily erected in the woods when villagers go out to hunt, or fish, or pursue agriculture.

They had chosen a charming spot in the woods, just upon the shores of the lake, which here had abrupt banks. Their mosquito-nets were hung up under the trees; every family had a fire built, and from the pots came a fragrant smell of plantain and fish cooking. The savour was very pleasant to me, for I was hungry.

Presently, Shimbouvenegani came up. He was rejoiced to see me, and thanked his friend Damagondai for bringing his white man to visit him.

The appearance of Shimbouvenegani was comical. He was between sixty and seventy years of age, and was quite lean. His only garment was a very dirty swallow-tailed coat, which certainly must have belonged to the time of my grandfather. The buttons were all gone. On his head he wore a broad beaver hat, which dated nearly as far back as the coat itself. The fur was entirely worn off, and the hat had a very seedy appearance. But the king seemed very proud when he made his appearance. He thought his costume was just the thing, and he looked loftily around, as if to say, "Am I not a fine-looking fellow?" And truly, though his dress did not amount to much according to our notions, I doubt not it had cost him several slaves.

He asked me how I liked his costume, at the same time taking one of the smaller tails in his hand and shaking it.

Presently, some large pots of palm-wine werebrought, with which all hands proceeded to celebrate my arrival. Damagondai and Shimbouvenegani soon got drunk, and swore to each other eternal friendship, and

Shimbouvenegani promised to give one of his daughters in marriage to Damagondai.

Meantime, Damagondai had presented me to his eldest son, Okabi, who resided in the village of Shimbouvenegani. Okabi arranged a nice little place for me, with branches of trees, and made a kind of bed for me. He then gave me his two wives to take care of me, and to cook for me.

I had a very agreeable time in hunting while I was with Shimbouvenegani. It was during my stay there that I discovered the *nshiego mbouvé*, of which I will speak by-and-by.

We also had a great crocodile hunt, which pleased the people very much, as they are extravagantly fond of the meat. Now and then during my travels, for lack of something better, I have been obliged to eat crocodiles. I have tried it in all sorts of ways—steaks, stews, boiled, and broth; but I must say I was never fond of it.

They killed more or fewer crocodiles every day at this village; but the negroes were so lazy that they were glad to have me go and save them the trouble. Moreover, the crocodile has not much meat on him; so that, though some were killed every day, the village was never sufficiently supplied.

We went in canoes. These canoes on the Anengue are of very singular construction. They are quite flat-bottomed, and of very light draught; many of them are about fifty feet long, with a breadth of not more than two feet, and a depth of ten to twelve inches. They are made of a single tree. They are ticklish craft. The oarsmen stand up and use paddles seven feet long, with which they can propel one of these canoes at a very good rate. They are, of course, easilycapsized, the gunwale being but a very few inches above the water; but they do not often tip over. What surprised me most was the way in which the negro paddlers stood up at their work all day without tiring.

The negroes on the Anengue hunt the crocodile both with guns and with a kind of harpoon. The vulnerable part of the animal is near the joints of his forelegs; and there they endeavour to wound it. Though so many are killed they do not decrease in numbers, nor, strange to say, do they seem to grow more wary. They were to be seen everywhere during the dry season; when the rainy season comes they disappear.

As we started out, we saw them swimming in all directions, and lying on the mud banks sunning themselves. They took no notice of our canoe at all. As we were to shoot them we were obliged to look for our prizes on the shore, for if killed in the water they sink and are lost. Presently we saw one immense fellow extended on the bank among some reeds. We approached cautiously. I took good aim and knocked him over. He struggled hard to get to the water, but his strength gave out ere he could reach it, and to our great joy he expired. We could not think of taking his body into our canoe, for he was nearly twenty feet long.

We killed another which measured eighteen feet. I never saw more savage-looking jaws; they were armed with most formidable rows of teeth and looked as though a man would scarcely be a mouthful for them.

We had brought another canoe along, and capsizing this upon the shore, we rolled the dead monsters into it and paddled off for the village. Then we returned to the olako.

During the heat of the day these animals retire to the reeds, where they lie sheltered. In the morning, and late in the afternoon, they come forth to seek their prey. They swim very silently, and scarcely make even a ripple on the water, though they move along quite rapidly. The motion of their paws in swimming is like those of a dog, over and over. They can remain quite still on the top of the water, where they may be seen watching for prey with their dull wicked-looking eyes. When they are swimming the head is the only part of the body visible; and when they are still, it looks exactly like an old piece of wood which has remained long in the water, and is tossing to and fro. They sleep among the reeds. Their eggs they lay in the sand on the island, and cover them over with a layer of sand. It is the great abundance of fish in the lake which makes them multiply so fast as they do. The negroes seemed rather indifferent to their presence.

On my journey back to Damagondai's I saw an example of the manner in which the crocodile seizes upon his prey. As we were paddling along I perceived in the distance ahead a beautiful gazelle, looking meditatively into the waters of the lagoon, of which from time to time it took a drink. I stood up to get a shot, and we approached with the utmost silence; but just as I raised my gun to fire a crocodile leaped out of the water, and, like a flash, dived back again, with the struggling animal in its powerful jaws. So quickly did the beast take its prey that, though I fired at him, I was too late. I did not think my bullet hit him.

After hunting on the water, I thought I would have a few rambles in the forest near the olako. I killed a beautiful monkey, which the natives call nkago, whose head is crowned with a cap of bright red, or ratherbrown, hair. The nkagos are very numerous in these woods.

While walking in the forest I found, near the water, the hole or burrow of an ogata. This is a species of cayman, which lives near the pools, and makes a long hole in the ground, with two entrances. In this hole it sleeps and watches for its prey. The ogata is very unlike the crocodile in its habits. It is a night-roving animal, and solitary in its ways. It scrapes out its hole with its paws with considerable labour. It lives near a pool, for the double reason, I imagine, that it may bathe, and because thither come gazelles and other animals, for whom it lies in wait. The negroes told me that they rush out with great speed upon any wandering animal, and drag it into the hole to eat it. When the negroes discover one of these holes they come with their guns, which are generally loaded with iron spikes, and watch at one end, while a fire is built at the other entrance. When it becomes too hot the ogata rushes out, and is shot. I killed one which proved to be seven feet in length. It had great strength in its jaws, and its teeth were very formidable. Like the crocodile, its upper jaw is articulated, and is raised when the mouth is opened.

Sometimes fire is put at both ends of the hole, and the animal is smoked to death. At other times a trap is made at the end where there is no fire, and when the ogata rushes out it is ensnared.

CHAPTER XXVIII.

THE NSHIEGO MBOUVÉ—BALD-HEADED APES—THEIR HOUSES IN THE TREES—LYING IN WAIT FOR THEM—WE KILL A MALE—THE SHRIEKS OF HIS MATE—DESCRIPTION OF THE ANIMAL—FAREWELL TO SHIMBOUVENEGANI.

AS I was trudging along one day in the woods, rather tired of the sport, and on the point of going back to the camp, I happened to look up at a high tree which we were passing and saw a most singular shelter or home built in its branches. I immediately stopped and asked Okabi why the hunters slept in that way in the woods. Okabi laughed, after looking at me quizzically, and then he told me that no man had ever built that shelter. He said that it was made by a kind of man of the woods, called nshiego mbouvé, an animal which had no hair on the top of its head. I really thought Okabi was joking. An animal—a man-monkey—with no hair on the top of his head? a bald-headed ape? It was now my turn to laugh, for I did not believe Okabi's story about the bald-headed animal, though I believed what he said about the shelter in the tree.

I saw at once that I was on the trail of an animal which no civilized man had ever seen before. I no longer felt tired, but pushed on through the woods with renewed ardour, and with increased caution, so as not to alarm our prey. The shelter we had seen was an old one, which had been abandoned, but we had a hope of finding another which should be still occupied.

We were not disappointed. We soon found two more shelters. They were about twenty feet from the ground, and were on two trees, which stood a little apart from the others, and which had no limbs below the one on which the nests were placed. This location for its house is probably chosen by the animals to secure them at night from beasts and serpents, and from the falling limbs of surrounding trees. They build only in the loneliest part of the forest. They are very shy, and are seldom seen, even by the negroes.

Okabi, who was an old and intelligent hunter, told me that the male and female together select the material for their nest or shelter. It is constructed in part of the branches of the tree itself, which they twist in with the boughs of other trees collected bythem for the purpose. The shelters I saw had the shape of an umbrella.

We concealed ourselves by lying flat on the ground amidst the bushes near by, and keeping perfectly still. My patience was sorely tried. Mosquitoes and flies were continually biting me. Ants now and then were creeping upon me, and some of them managed to get under my clothes. Besides, I had some fear of the bashikonay, or of the white ants, coming to disturb me, or of snakes creeping upon me. So, as you may imagine, I was not comfortable, neither had I pleasant thoughts.

At length, just at dusk, we heard the loud peculiar "hew, hew, hew," which is the call of the male to his mate. I was glad to know I had not waited in vain; and looking up I saw a nshiego mbouvé sitting under his nest. His feet rested on the lower branch; his head reached quite into the little dome of a roof; and his arm was clasped firmly about the tree trunk. This, I suppose, is the position in which they sleep. Soon after his mate came and ascended the tree.

After gazing till I was tired, I saw that one of the animals showed signs of being alarmed. Had they smelt us? had we made a noise that excited their suspicions? Anyhow, we raised our guns and fired through the gloom at the one that seemed asleep. I almost felt sorry for the unfortunate beast, which fell with a tremendous crash, and died without a struggle. The other uttered an awful shriek and came down the tree with the utmost rapidity. I fired but missed the animal, and in less time than I take to write it the poor creature had disappeared in the woods.

I was very hungry, for I had eaten nothing since breakfast. We built a fire at once, and made our camp. Then we built several more fires, to prevent an attack of the bashikonay ants, in case they shouldcome that way. The poor ape was hung up to a limb out of reach. During the night, I could hear now and then, in the distance, the piercing shriek of its mate, which no doubt was calling for the absent one. At last I fell asleep on my bed of leaves and grass, as pleased a man perhaps as any in the world.

The next morning I examined the nshiego mbouvé. Okabi, pointing to the head triumphantly, exclaimed, "See, Chaillie, is not the animal bald-headed? Did I not tell you the truth?" So it was. The nshiego mbouvé was quite bald; not a hair could be seen on the top of his head. He was a full-grown specimen, and measured three feet and eleven inches in height. His colour was intensely black, and the body was covered with short, rather blackish hair. On the legs the hair was of a dirty grey, mixed with black. On the shoulders and back the hair grew two or three inches long. This animal was old, and his hair was a little mixed with grey. The arms also, down to the wrists, were covered with long black hair. The hair is much thinner than on the gorilla, and is blacker, longer, and glossier. The nose, also, is not so prominent. Though only three feet and eleven inches in height, the animal had an extremely broad chest, though not so powerful as that of the gorilla. The fingers, also, were much longer, and not large; and the hand was longer than the foot; while the gorilla, like man, has the foot longer than the hand.

Some of the teeth were decayed. So the poor fellow must have had the toothache badly; and I suppose there were no dentists among the nshiego mbouvés. I have killed several of these animals. One of them was a very old one; he had silvery hair; nearly all his teeth were decayed, and some were missing which had dropped out with age. He was getting so infirm that he had not strength enough to pickberries or break nuts; and, when killed, he had only leaves in his stomach.

After enjoying myself thoroughly at the olako of Shimbouvenegani, we returned to the village of Damagondai. Shimbouvenegani dressed himself again in state, that is to say, he put on his swallow-tailed coat and his beaver hat. In this regal costume he accompanied us to our canoes, and there bid us good-bye.

CHAPTER XXIX.

WAR THREATENED—OSHORIA ARMS HIS MEN—WE BLUFF THEM OFF, AND FALL SICK WITH FEVER—THE MBOLA IVOGA, OR END OF MOURNING TIME—A DEATH AND BURIAL—FINDING OUT THE SORCERER—THE VILLAGE DESERTED—I BECOME VICEROY AT WASHINGTON.

News came that Oshoria, the chief of Guabuirri, a village situated at the junction of the Ogobai and Anengue rivers, intended to stop me on my way back to Washington. It was reported that he had assembled all his fighting men, and was bent upon war.

Poor Damagondai was much troubled. He wanted no war. He sent his brother down with a plate, a mug, and a brass pan, to propitiate Oshoria. These were great presents. A plate, a mug, and a pan are thought to be very valuable in the regions of the Anengue.

I was very angry. I had done no harm to the people of Guabuirri; I had passed their village in peace. Oshoria wanted to exact tribute for my passage; but he was not the king of the country, and I determined to put down Mr. Oshoria.

We cleaned our guns, and I prepared my revolvers, and the next morning we set out, without waiting for the return of the king's brother, greatly to the dismay of Damagondai and of his peaceful people. But nothing must stop us. We must return to Washington. My men swore that they would fight to the death.

When we came in sight of Guabuirri, I saw that some of my fellows, who, a short time before, were going to be so brave, began to show the white feather. I therefore pointed to my revolver, and told them that I would blow out the brains of the first man who failed to fight to the last. They had a great respect for this wonderful revolver, and they immediately answered, "We are men."

So we pulled down the stream and soon came almost opposite Oshoria's people. I gave orders to make for the town. On the shore stood about one hundred and fifty fellows armed with spears and axes, and led by ten men who had guns. All of them were making a great noise.

My men were all well armed, and, if I remember well, there were only sixteen of us. I had my revolver in one hand and a double-barrelled gun in the other. The men all had guns, which were placed beside them in such a way that the natives on the shore could seethem. At this piece of bravado, Oshoria's men became very civil. They retreated as we approached the landing; and instead of continuing their war-shouts and firing at us, they received us peaceably, and shouted to us not to fire.

Damagondai's brother hurried down to meet me, and announced that there was no palaver: I must not kill anybody. I was then led to where the quarrelsome Oshoria stood. Looking at him with a stern look, I reproached him for his conduct, telling him that if anybody had been killed, the palaver would have been on his own head. He said he had been vexed that I did not stop to see him on my way up; and, after making further excuses, added, "Aouè olomé," "thou art a man;" an expression used in several ways, either to designate a smart man or a rascal, or, in the best sense, a very brave man. I was content to accept it as an intended compliment.

I was presented with fruits and fowls, and we were presently the best of friends. To show them what I could do in the way of shooting, I brought down a little bird which sat on a very high tree. They all declared that I must have a very big shooting fetich; and they reverenced me greatly.

The next morning, I left Oshoria, and once more I glided down the placid waters of the Ogobai. I reached Washington in safety.

It was in the month of August, and the malaria of the Anengue marshes began to tell on me. I fell sick with dysentery and symptoms of malignant fever. In three days I took one hundred and eighty grains of quinine, and thus happily succeeded in breaking the force of the fever, which was the most dangerous of the two diseases. I was ill from the 18th to the 31st of August; and I did not regain my strength till the 9th of September. The Commi waited patiently for my recovery before they would go through some of then ceremonies.

There was to be a *mbola ivoga* at Biagano, that is, an end of the mourning time, to be celebrated with ceremonies and a terrible noise.

When anyone of importance dies, the clan, or town, or the relatives, cease to wear their best clothes, and make it a point to go unusually dirty. No ornaments whatever, such as earrings or bracelets or beads, are worn. This is the way they "mourn." Mourning lasts generally from one year to two years. The ceremonies at the breaking-up of this mourning are what I am now about to describe.

The man who had died left seven wives, a house, a plantation, several slaves, and other property. All this the elder brother inherited; and on him, as the heir, it devolved to give the grand feast. For this feast every canoe that came brought jars of mimbo, or palm-wine. Sholomba and Jombouai, the heir, with his people, had been out for two weeks, fishing, and now returned with several canoe-loads of dry fish. From his plantation a large supply of palm-wine was brought in. The women and slaves had prepared a great quantity of food. Everything needful was provided in great abundance.

In the village the people all got ready their best clothes and furbished up their ornaments. Drums and kettles were collected for music; powder was brought out for the salutes; and at last all was ready for the mbola ivoga.

The seven wives of the deceased seemed quite jolly, for to-morrow they were to lay aside their widows' robes, and to join in the jollification as brides. The heir could have married them all; but he had generously given up two to a younger brother, and one to a cousin. He had already sixteen wives, and mightwell be content with only four more. Twenty wives is a pretty good number.

No wonder the widows were glad to see the time of mourning over. For two whole years they had been almost imprisoned in their husband's house, hardly ever going out.

At seven o'clock three guns were fired off, to announce that the widows had done eating a certain mess, mixed of various ingredients, supposed to have magical virtues, and by which they are released from their widowhood. This was the first part of the ceremony. They then put on bracelets and anklets, and the finest calico they had. Some of the Commi women wear brass anklets on each leg almost as high as the knee, as you see represented in the picture. The weight must be between twenty and thirty pounds on each leg. Besides these anklets, they wear a few bracelets of the same material. On their necks they wear beads.

From early morning the guests had been coming, all bringing provisions and mimbo (palm-wine) with them, and dressed in their best clothes. There were several hundreds in all. The guests that lived far away had come the day before. About nine o'clock all the guests sat down on mats, spread about outside of the house of the deceased, and along the main street. They were divided into little groups; and before each was set an immense jar of mimbo, and food was spread before them. All began to talk pleasantly, till, suddenly, the Biagano people fired off a volley of about one hundred guns. This was the signal for the drinking and eating to begin. Men, women, and children set to, and ate as much as they could; and from this time till the next morning the orgies were continued without interruption. They drank, they sang, they shouted, they fired guns, and loaded them so heavily when they got tipsy that I wonder the old trade-guns did not burst. They drummed on everything that could possibly give out a noise. The women danced—such dances as are not seen elsewhere! You may imagine what they were, when every woman was so furiously tipsy.

This mbola ivoga would have lasted probably for several days, but the victuals and palm-wine finally gave out.

Next day, about sunrise, Jombouai came and asked me to assist at the concluding ceremony; for I had told him that I wanted to see every scene of the mbola ivoga. His brother's house, according to the custom, was to be torn down and burned—yes, burned to the ground, so that not a vestige of it would remain to remind the people that once there stood a house whose possessor was dead.

The people came around the house and fired guns; then, in a moment, as if they were an infuriated mob, they hacked the old house to pieces with axes and cutlasses; then they set fire to it. When the ruins were burnt, the feast was done.

This is the way they go out of mourning among the Commi. The widows were all married again, and, until another death should occur, everything would go smoothly again.

Hardly were the rejoicings over, when Ishungui, the man who had faithfully taken care of my house in my absence, lay at death's door. He had gone out on Jombouai's fishing excursion, in order to catch fish for the mbola ivoga which I have just described. He caught cold, and had now a lung fever. The people called for me. I knew as soon as I saw him that he must die, and I tried to prepare his mind for the change. But his friends and relatives by no means gave him up. They sent for a distinguished fetich doctor, and under his auspices they began the infernal din with which they seek to cure a dying man. I am afraid the cure is worse than the disease.

One of the Commi people's theories of disease is, that Obambou (the devil) has got into the sick man, and as long as the devil remains in the body there is no hope of curing the man. Now this devil is only to be driven out by noise, and accordingly a great crowd surround the sick man and beat drums and kettles close to his head, fire off guns close to his ears, and in every part of the house they sing, shout, dance, and make all the noise they can. This lasts till the poor fellow either dies or is better; but I must say that he generally dies, unless the operators get tired out first.

Ishungui died. He left no property, and his brother buried him in the sand, without a coffin, in a grave so shallow (as is the custom) that, when I came upon it some days after, I saw that the wild beasts had been there and eaten the corpse.

The mourning was short in this case; it lasted only six days. There were no wives or property; there was no feast. The relatives of the deceased slept one night in his house, as a mark of respect.

Among the Commi it is the custom, when a man has died, to keep the *nchougou*. The nchougou is a feast that takes place generally, if not always, after the man has been dead six days. There is drinking, eating, and dancing; but the rejoicing is not so uproarious as the ceremony of the mbola ivoga. Then the mourning begins. I think you will agree with me that the nchougou is a most extraordinary custom.

After Ishungui had died, it became necessary to discover the persons who had bewitched the dead man; for the Commi said, "How is it that a young man, generally healthy, should die so suddenly?" This they did not believe to be natural; hence theyattributed his death to sorcerers, and were afraid that the sorcerers would kill other people.

A canoe had been despatched up to Lake Anengue to bring down a great doctor. They brought down one of Damagondai's sons, a great rascal. He had been foremost in selling me the idol, or *mbuiti*, of the slaves of which I spoke to you, and he was an evident cheat.

When all was ready for the trial, I went down to look at the doctor, who looked really diabolical. I never saw a more ugly-looking object.

He had on a high head-dress of black feathers. His eyelids were painted red, and a red stripe, from the nose upward, divided his forehead into two parts; another stripe passed around his head. The face was painted white, and on each side of the mouth were two round red spots. About his neck hung a necklace of grass, and also a cord, which held a box against his breast. This little box is sacred, and contains spirits. A number of strips of leopard's skin, and of skin of other animals, crossed his breast, and were exposed about his person; and all these were charmed and had charms attached to them. From each shoulder down to his hands was a white stripe, and one hand was painted quite white. To complete this horrible array, he wore around his body a string of little bells.

He sat on a box. Before him stood another box containing charms. On this stood a looking-glass, before which lay a buffalo-horn. In this horn there was some black powder, and it was said to be the refuge of many spirits. The doctor had also a little basket of snake-bones, which he shook frequently during his incantations, and several skins, to which little bells were attached. Near by stood a fellow beating a board with two sticks.

All the people of the village gathered about this couple. The doctor had, no doubt, impressed thepeople with his great power. His incantations were continued for a long time, and at last came to the climax. Jombouai was told to call over the names of persons in the village, in order that the doctor might ascertain if any of those named were sorcerers. As each name was called, the old cheat looked in the looking-glass to see the result.

During the whole operation I stood near him, which seemed to trouble him greatly. At last, after all the names were called, the doctor declared that he could not find any "witch-man," but that an evil spirit dwelt in the village, and many of the people would die if it continued there. I have a suspicion that this final judgment with which the incantations broke up was a piece of revenge upon me. I had no idea until the next day how seriously the word of one of these *ougangas* (doctors) is taken.

The next morning all was excitement. The people were scared. They said their mbuiti was not willing to have them live longer here; that he would kill them, etc. Then began the removal of all kinds of property, and the tearing down of houses, and by nightfall I was actually left alone in my house with a Mpongwe boy and my little Ogobai boy, Macondai, both of whom were anxious to be off.

Old Ranpano came to beg me not to be offended; he said that he dared not stay; that the mbuiti was now in town. He advised me as a friend to move also; but nobody wished me ill, only he must go, and would build his house not far off.

I did not like to abandon my house and settlement at Washington, which it had cost me a good deal of trouble to build. I called a meeting of the people, and it was with the greatest difficulty that I could get some of my own canoe boys and a few men to come and stay at my place. These began immediately to build themselves houses, and a little village was built, of which I was now, to my great surprise, offered the sovereignty. I remembered how the new king was made in the Gaboon, and I did not know but that the Commi had the same custom. The thought of the ceremony which precedes the assumption of royalty deterred me. Finally, the men determined to have me as their chief, next to Ranpano; and with this my ambition was satisfied.

CHAPTER XXX.

HUNTING IN THE WOODS—THE MBOYO WOLF—WE CATCH ANOTHER YOUNG GORILLA—HE STARVES TO DEATH.

Everything went on smoothly among the good Commi. When I absented myself they took great care of my property. They seemed proud of their honesty; and though it was a wild country, and they were a wild people, I felt very safe among them.

Now and then I left Washington to go and live entirely in the woods, and hunt, sometimes for gorillas, at other times for wild boars or buffaloes, or something else.

I was also very fond of hunting the *mboyo*, a very shy animal of the wolf kind, with long yellowish hair and straight ears. They are very cunning; and now and then you can see them in the grass engaged in hunting for themselves. I have often watched these animals surrounding and chasing game. They run very well together in a drove; and as their policy is to run round and round, they soon bewilder, tire out, and capture any animal of moderate endurance. As they run round, gradually their circle grows smaller and smaller; and of course the smaller it becomes the more bewildered becomes their prey.

Often I have seen them prying about alone in search of prey. How roguish they look! and I could only shoot them at very long distances. I never was able to get near one of them.

At times I went into the country where gorillas were plentiful, and had a good deal of fun and plenty of excitement. This country was not far from the village of a chief called Makaga Oune-jiou. This chief was affected with leprosy. He had already lost all the fingers of his left hand and two fingers of his right hand, besides the big toe of his left foot. But Makaga was very kind to me, and was much beloved by his people. His village was small, but was a very dear little village to him. It was surrounded by fields of sugar-cane, plantain trees, and little fields of ground-nuts; and now and then the gorillas came and helped themselves to the good things these people had planted. This made them very wroth, and they were always glad to have me come and spend a few days among them.

Early in the morning I could sometimes hear the gorillas, who then came quite near the village. Here I found that I need not make long journeys in order toreach the hunting ground. But they are difficult of approach; the slightest noise alarms them and sends them off. It is only once in a while that you can surprise an old male, and then he will fight you.

While staying with Makaga Oune-jiou I captured a second young gorilla; and we had an exciting time, I assure you, before we got him.

We were walking along in silence, when I heard a cry, and presently I saw not far from me, in the midst of a dense foliage, a female gorilla, with a tiny baby gorilla hanging to her breast. The mother was stroking the little one, and looking fondly down at it; and the scene was so pretty and touching that I withheld my fire and considered (like a soft-hearted fellow) whether I had not better leave them in peace. Before I could make up my mind, however, my hunter fired and killed the mother, who fell dead without a struggle.

The mother fell, but the baby clung to her, and, with piteous cries, endeavoured to attract her attention. I came up, and when it saw me it hid its poor little head in its mother's breast. It could neither walk nor bite, it was such a tiny little baby gorilla. We could easily manage it; and I carried it, while the men bore the mother on a pole.

When we got to the village another scene ensued. The men put the body down, and I set the little fellow near. As soon as he saw his mother he crawled to her and threw himself on her breast. He did not find his accustomed nourishment, and perceived that something was the matter with his mother. He crawled over her body, smelt at it, and gave utterance from time to time to a plaintive cry, "Hoo, hoo, hoo," which touched my heart.

I could get no milk for this poor little fellow. He could not eat, and consequently he died on the third day after he was caught.

CHAPTER XXXI.

GOING TO UNKNOWN REGIONS—QUENGUEZA SENDS HIS
SON AS A HOSTAGE—I TAKE HIM ALONG WITH ME—
RECEPTION BY THE KING—OUR SPEECHES—QUENGUEZA
AFRAID OF A WITCH—AN INCANTATION SCENE.

Time passed on. It was several years since I left the United States, but
nevertheless I determined to set out for the head waters of the Fernand-
Vaz, and for countries undiscovered as yet by white men.

Quengueza had sent to me his eldest son, namedKombé (the sun), with a
present of ebony wood, and his youngest son, a boy of ten, called Akounga;
and he said I must come and leave Akounga in Ranpano's hands as a
hostage for my safety. "You see," he sent word, "that I am not afraid of
you. You may trust me."

I had to take my big boat, because no canoe would hold all the goods,
powder and shot, guns, provisions, and medicines, I took along. It was to
be a very, very long journey. I was the first white man to venture up in this
direction, and I was anxious to get as far as possible.

We were fifteen in all in my boat. Another canoe, with fifteen more men,
followed us. Quengueza's little boy was with us too. I would never have
thought of such a thing as keeping the poor little fellow away from his
mother and father. I took also the brave little Macondai, whom I had at
first determined to leave behind, as being too small to stand the fatigues of
such a journey. The little fellow entreated so much to be taken that I at last
consented. He behaved like a man. Macondai grew fast as years went by,
and I wish you could have seen him fighting by my side in Ashango land.

At last, after much fatigue and hard pulling, we reached the village of
Goumbi, the residence of King Quengueza. Here I was received in the
most triumphant manner. I could not make myself heard for the shouts and
firing of guns. The whole population of Goumbi crowded down to the
shore to see me, and I was led up in procession to an immense covered
space, capable of holding at least a thousand people, and surrounded by
seats. I found there strangers from various parts of the interior, who gazed
at me, and especially at my hair, with the greatest wonder.

A large high seat was appointed for me, and anotherclose to it was for
Quengueza, who presently arrived with a face beaming with joy. He shook
hands with me and then seated himself.

There was a dead silence in the vast crowd before us. Quengueza was an
old, white-woolled negro, very tall, spare, and of a severe countenance,

betokening great energy and courage, qualities for which he was celebrated all over their country. When younger he was the dread of all, but now that he had become the chief of his clan, and was getting old, he had grown milder, and become peaceful, to the great joy of the surrounding villages. He was a very remarkable man for his opportunities. He made haste to tell me that he was in mourning for his eldest brother, who had died two years before, and left him chief of their clan, the Abouya.

Quengueza had on a finely-knit black cap, and a grass body-cloth, which was black also; both the cap and cloth were of Ashira make, and were really beautiful. He had no shirt; that article is not allowed to mourners; but he wore an American coat which was too small for him.

After the king had done welcoming me, I called his little son, Akounga. When he had come forward, I said to the king in a loud voice, that the people might hear: "You sent your son to me to keep, so that I might feel safe to come to you. I am not afraid. I like you, and can trust you. Therefore I have brought your little son back to you. I do not want him as a hostage for my safety. Let him remain by the side of his mother."

At this there was a tremendous shouting, and the people seemed overjoyed.

The king rose to reply. There was immediately a dead silence; for Quengueza was greatly reverenced by his people. The king said: "This is my *ntangani*(white man), he has come from a far country to see me. I went down to beg him to come up to me. Now he has come. Let no one do harm to his people; for him I need not speak. Give food to his people. Treat them well. Do not steal anything. If you do not do as I say, A BIG PALAVER WILL COME UPON YOU!" This last sentence he uttered in a tremendous voice.

Then he addressed himself to the Ashira and Bakalai who were present, saying,: "Beware! Do not steal my white man, for if you should make the attempt, I will sell you all."

Then loads of plantains and sugar-canes, together with a hundred fowls, and several goats, were presented to me by the king, and this closed the ceremony.

The longer I stayed with Quengueza, the more I loved him; I was only sorry that he was so curiously superstitious. For a year he had not passed down the street which led most directly to the water, but had gone always by a roundabout way, because, when he came to the throne, this street was pronounced bewitched by a secret enemy of his; and he was persuaded that if he passed by it, he would surely die. This superstitious notion had originated in a dream of the king's which had been interpreted in that way.

Several times efforts had been made by distinguished doctors to drive away the *aniemba* (witch), which there lay in wait; but the king, though he believed in sorcery, did not have much faith in the exorcisers or doctors. He thought that, perhaps, the aniemba had not gone, and that it was better to be on the safe side, which was not to go on the road at all. But his subjects felt very much troubled about this matter; for they wanted their king to pass through their street sometimes.

Once more a last attempt was made to drive off theaniemba, or witch. A famous doctor from the far-off Bakalai country had been brought down to perform this act. His name was Aquailai.

In the evening the people gathered in great numbers under the immense *hangar*, or covered space in which I had been received, and there lit fires, around which they sat. The space thus covered was one hundred and fifty feet long by forty wide, and was roofed with palm branches and leaves.

About ten o'clock, when it was pitch dark, the doctor commenced operations by singing some boastful songs, recounting his power over witches. Immediately all the people gathered into their houses, and with such great haste, that two women failing to get home, and afraid to go farther through the streets, took refuge in my house. Then all the fires in the houses were carefully extinguished, those under the hangar having been already put out; and, in about an hour more, there was not a light of any kind in the whole town except mine. They had only asked of me that I should shut my door. The most pitchy darkness and the most complete silence reigned everywhere. No voice could be heard, even in a whisper, among the several thousands of people gathered in the gloom.

At last the silence was broken by the doctor, who, standing in the centre of the town, began some loud babbling, of which I could not make out the meaning. From time to time the people answered him in chorus. This went on for an hour, and was really one of the strangest scenes I ever took part in. I could see nothing but the faces of the two women in my house, who were badly frightened, poor things, as, in fact, all the people were. The hollow voice of the witch-doctor resounded curiously through the silence; and when the answer of many mingled voices came throughthe darkness, the ceremony really assumed the air of a poet's incantation scene.

At last, just at midnight by my watch, I heard the doctor approach. He had bells girded about him, which he jingled as he walked. He went to every family in the town, successively, and asked if to them belonged the aniemba (witch) that obstructed the king's highway. Of course, all answered no. Then he began to run up and down the bewitched street, calling out loudly for the witch to go off. Presently he came back and announced that he could no longer see the aniemba, which had doubtless gone, never to come back. At this, all the people rushed out of their houses, and shouted, "Go away! go away! and never come back to hurt our king!"

Then fires were lit, and all sat down to eat. This done, all the fires were once more extinguished; and the people sung wild songs until four o'clock. Then the fires were lit again.

At sunrise the whole population gathered to accompany their king down the dreaded street to the water. Quengueza, I know, was brave as a hunter and as a warrior. He was also very intelligent about many things regarding which his people were very stupid; but the poor old king was now horribly afraid. He was assured that the aniemba was gone; but he evidently thought that he was walking to almost certain death. He hesitated; but at last he determined to face his fate, and walked manfully down to the river and back, amidst the plaudits of his loyal subjects. So ended the ceremony; but Quengueza never went again on that road; his dread of it still remained.

CHAPTER XXXII.

GORILLA HUNTING—MY COMPANIONS, MOMBON, ETIA, AND GAMBO—ETIA KILLS A LARGE GORILLA—WE MAKE UP A LARGE PARTY—CAMP STORIES ABOUT GORILLAS—WE CAPTURE A YOUNG GORILLA—HER UNTIMELY DEATH.

Quengueza had a slave named Mombon, whom he loved greatly. Mombon was his overseer, chamberlain, steward, man of business, and general factotum, the man whose place it was to take care of the king's private affairs, set his slaves to work, oversee his plantations, and who had the care of the keys of the royal houses. Mombon was to see that I was made comfortable in town.

Quengueza had also another slave named Etia. Etia was his favourite hunter, and he gave him to me for a guide in the bush. This Etia was a fine-looking old man, belonging to a tribe far in the interior, who had never heard that there was such a thing as a whiteman in the world. He was living on a little plantation outside the town, where he had a neat house and a nice old wife, who always treated me in a kind, motherly way; she always had something to give me to eat. Etia's business was to supply the royal larder with "bush meat," and he went out hunting almost every week for that purpose.

Etia and I became great friends, and loved each other much. I gave to Etia and to his wife many little presents, with which they always seemed very much pleased. Around the house of Etia were arranged skulls of elephants, hippopotami, leopards, and gorillas, as trophies of his prowess.

Among the numerous guests of Quengueza was an Ashira chief, who had come on a visit to the king. He had a son called Gambo, a noted hunter. Gambo was a very ill-looking fellow, but he had a fiery eye, great courage, and a kind heart. I became very fond of Gambo, and Gambo became very fond of me. Sometimes Quengueza could not help saying to his people, "See how hunters love each other, no matter if they come from different countries. See how my white man loves the black hunters." In fact, we were always together. I had never seen the Ashira tribe to which Gambo belonged.

One day we had been going through the woods about three hours when at last we came upon fresh gorilla tracks. Etia now set out alone, while Gambo and I walked silently in another direction. The gorilla is so difficult to approach that we had literally to creep through the thick woods when in their vicinity. The hunter cannot expect to see his enemy till he is close upon him. The forest is so thick and gloomy that even when quite near the animal is but dimly visible. All this makes hunting for the gorilla very trying to the nerves; for it is in the hunter's mind that if he misses —if his bullet does not go to the most fatal point—the wounded and infuriated brute will make short work of his opponent.

As we crept silently along, suddenly the woods resounded with the report of a gun. We sped at once towards the quarter whence the report came, and there we found old Etia sitting complacently upon the dead body of the largest female gorilla I ever saw. The total height of the animal was four feet seven inches. This was a huge gorilla for a female, for they are always much smaller than the males.

Another time we made up a large party. We were to go a considerable distance to a spot where Etia gave me hopes that we should catch a young gorilla alive. I would have gone through any hardship and peril to get one large enough to be kept alive, and to be sent to Europe.

Etia, Gambo, myself, and ten men composed our party. Each was armed, and laden with provisions for a couple of days. The men were covered with fetiches. They had painted their faces red, and had cut their hands in more than fifty different places. This bleeding of the hands was done for luck. The fellows were nearly naked; but this is their usual habit.

As for me, I had also made extra preparations. I had blackened my face and hands with powdered charcoal and oil; and my blue drilling shirt and trousers and black shoes made me as dark as any of them. My revolvers hung at my side, with my ammunition bag and brandy flask; my rifle lay upon my shoulder. All this excited the admiration of the crowd which assembled to see us go out.

Quengueza was greatly delighted, and exclaimed, "What kind of ntangani (white man) is this? He fears nothing; he cares for neither sun nor water; he loves nothing but the hunt."

The old king charged the people to take great care of his white man, and to defend him with their lives if need be.

We travelled all day, and about sunset we came to a little river. Here we began at once to make a fire and build leafy shelters for the night. Scarcely was the firewood gathered, and we were safely bestowed under our shelter, when a storm came up which lasted half an hour. Then all was clear once more. We cooked plantains and smoked some dried fishes.

In the evening the men told stories about gorillas.

"I remember," said one, "my father told me he once went out to the forest, when just in his path he met a great gorilla. My father had his spear in his hand. When the gorilla saw the spear he began to roar; then my father was terrified, and dropped the spear. When the gorilla saw that my father had dropped the spear he was pleased. He looked at him, and then left him and went into the thick forest. Then my father was glad, and went on his way."

Here all shouted together, "Yes! so we must do when we meet the gorilla. Drop the spear; that appeases him."

Next Gambo spoke. "Several dry seasons ago a man suddenly disappeared from my village after an angry quarrel. Some time after an Ashira of that village was out in the forest. He met a very large gorilla. That gorilla was the man who had disappeared; he had turned into a gorilla. He jumped on the poor Ashira and bit a piece out of his arm. Then he let him go. Then the man came back with his bleeding arm. He told me this. I hope we shall not meet such gorillas."

Chorus—"No; we shall not meet such wicked gorillas."

I myself afterwards met that man in the Ashiracountry. I saw his maimed arm, and he repeated the same story.

Then one of the men spoke up: "If we kill a gorilla to-morrow I should like to have a part of the brain for a fetich. Nothing makes a man so brave as to have a fetich of gorilla's brain. That gives a man a strong heart."

Chorus of those who remained awake—"Yes; that gives a man a strong heart."

Then we all gradually dropped to sleep.

Next morning we cleaned and reloaded our guns, and started off for the hunting ground. There is a particular little berry of which the gorilla is very fond, and where this is found in abundance you are sure to meet the animal.

We had divided. Etia, Gambo, two other men, and I kept together, and we had hardly gone more than an hour when we heard the cry of a young gorilla after his mother. Etia heard it first, and at once pointed out the direction in which it was.

Immediately we began to walk with greater caution than before. Presently Etia and Gambo crept ahead, as they were expert with the net, and were also the best woodsmen. I unwillingly remained behind, but dared not go with them, lest my clumsier movements should betray our presence. In a short time we heard two guns fired. Running up, we found the mother gorilla shot, but her little one had escaped; they had not been able to catch it.

The poor mother lay there in her gore, but the little fellow was off in the woods. So we concealed ourselves hard by to wait, for its return. Presently it came up, jumped on its mother, and began sucking at her breasts and fondling her. Then Etia, Gambo, and I rushed upon it. Though evidently less than two years old, it proved very strong, and escaped from us. But we gave chase, and in a few minutes had it fast, not, however, before one of the men had his arm severely bitten by the savage little beast.

It proved to be a young female. Unhappily, she lived but ten days after capture. She persistently refused to eat any cooked food, or anything else except the nuts and berries which they eat in the forest. She was not so ferocious as "Fighting Joe," but was quite as treacherous and quite as untameable. She permitted no one to approach her without trying to bite. Her eyes seemed somewhat milder than Joe's, but had the same gloomy and treacherous look, and she had the same way as Joe of looking you straight in the eyes when she was meditating an attack. I remarked in her also the same manœuvre practised by the other when she wished to seize something, my leg, for instance, which, by reason of the chain around her neck, she could not reach with her arm. She would look me straight in the face, then quick as a flash would throw her body on one leg and one arm and reach out with the other leg. Several times I had narrow escapes from the grip of her strong big toe. I thought sometimes that when she looked at me she appeared cross-eyed, but of this I could not make certain. All her motions were remarkably quick, and her strength was very great, though she was so small.

CHAPTER XXXIII.

VOYAGE UP THE RIVER—WE BUILD A VILLAGE NEAR OBINDJI—QUENGUEZA'S PLAN FOR KEEPING THE SABBATH—KINDNESS OF THE NATIVES—A TRIAL BY ORDEAL.

King Quengueza accompanied me on my voyage up the Rembo and Ovenga rivers. We were followed by a great many canoes, and by chiefs of the Ashira and Bakalai tribes. We were going to the Bakalai country. The weather was intensely hot; even the negroes suffered; and, though I had a thick umbrella over my head, and sat quitestill, I had frequently to bathe my head and keep wet handkerchiefs in my banana hat; for I feared a sunstroke.

The river was narrow and deep, flowing generally between high lands and hills, and now and then in the midst of flats.

Everybody complained except Macondai. He was the most spirited little negro I ever saw, a real little hero. I tell you that many, very many, of these African boys have a good deal of pluck, although they are black.

Two days after we started, we arrived, a little before sunset, at the village of Obindji, a Bakalai chief, who was a great friend of Quengueza. Wherever we passed a Bakalai village the people rushed down to the banks to see me. As we approached the village of Obindji, our men fired guns and sang songs. Obindji came down in great state, dressed in his silk hat, a shirt, and a nice cloth. He was ringing his *kendo*—a bell, which is the insignia of kingship there—a sort of royal sceptre. The high-crowned silk hat, also, as I said before, is worn only by the chiefs.

I said to Obindji, "Why do you ring your kendo?"

He replied, "Obindji's heart is glad, and he thanks his Mboundji (a spirit) that he has to-day come up higher than he ever stood before—a *ntanga* (white man) has come to see Obindji."

When we had landed, and the two kings and I were seated on the stools used in that country, the grand reception began. Quengueza gave to his friend Obindji, and to all the Bakalai who surrounded us, an account of his entire intercourse with me, from the time he came down to see me at the seashore to the present hour.

Then Obindji replied, giving, in like manner (in short sentences), a statement of his feelings when he heardthat Quengueza was to bring a ntanga to see him. This closed the conference.

The village of Obindji was small, and was beautifully situated at the foot of a high hill, just on the banks of the Ovenga. The Ovenga river belonged to Quengueza, and, except at its head waters, it had been inhabited by the Bakalai only since the time of Quengueza's eldest brother, whom he had succeeded. These Bakalai are very warlike; they are much dreaded by the other tribes.

The region of the Ovenga is a grand and wild country. It consists of hills and mountains, covered with impenetrable forests, which teem with all kinds of insects. Many animals, curious birds, and a great number of snakes are found there, together with those extraordinary ants—the bashikonay. There also are the chimpanzees and gorillas.

As I intended to remain some time, I set about building another village. The men all went into the forest to collect bark, palm leaves, and posts.

When Sunday came, I requested Quengueza to make the men rest on this day, explaining to him that white men do not work on the Sabbath.

The old man was puzzled for a moment, and then said, "We are much hurried now. Suppose you put off the Sunday for three or four weeks. Then we can have as many Sundays as you want. We will keep four or five days following each other as Sundays. It will be just the same."

He seemed quite proud of his discovery and was quite disappointed when I told him it would not do.

I worked very hard in building my house. The labour was the more trying because the heat was so intense; there was not a breath of wind in this Bakalai country. Besides, the fever had got hold of me again; but I did not give way to it.

Obindji became very friendly to me. I may say that all these negroes seemed to take a liking for me. I made quite a number of friends among the Bakalai. Two of them, indeed, were very dear friends of mine; they were called Malaouen and Querlaouen. I really do not know which of the two I liked the best. They were ready to do anything I wished them to do. If I proposed a hunt, they immediately offered to accompany me; if they killed game, they presented me with the best piece. Their wives were sure to bring me, almost every day, sugar-cane, plantain, or something else. As for Obindji, he did all in his power to please me. Moreover, Quengueza was always close to me. He said that wherever I went he would follow me, and build his shed by the side of mine. I was now Quengueza's white man and Obindji's white man. They all seemed to take pride in me. I am sure I also tried my best to be kind to them. Above all things, I wanted them to believe my word implicitly. Hence, whatever I promised, I kept my word. They noticed this; and therefore no one doubted me. These poor people, though they have no word to describe "an honest man," know the difference between lying and truth-telling; and they appreciate truthfulness.

One day I saw a trial by ordeal performed. A little boy, a son of Aquailai, the doctor who had driven the aniemba, or witch, from the main street at Goumbi, reported that one of Quengueza's men had damaged a Bakalai's canoe. The owner demanded compensation for the injury. The Goumbi men denied that he had injured the canoe, and asked for trial. An Ashira doctor who was in the village was called. He said that the only way to make the truth appear was by the trial of the ring boiled in oil. Thereupon, the Bakalai and the Goumbi men gathered together, and the trial was at once made.

The Ashira doctor stuck three little billets of wood into the ground, with their top ends together, then he piled some smaller pieces between, till all were laid as high as the three pieces. A native earthenware pot, half full of palm oil, was set upon the wood, which had been set on fire; and the oil was set on fire also. When it had burned up brightly, a brass bracelet or ring from the doctor's hand was cast into the pot. The doctor stood by with a little vase full of grass soaked in water, of which he threw in, now and then, some bits. This made the oil blaze up fresh. At last, all was burned out, and now came the trial. The accuser, the little boy, was required at once to take the ring out of the pot. He hesitated, but was pushed on by his father. The people cried out, "Let us see whether he lied or told the truth." Finally he put his hand in and seized the almost red-hot ring, but quickly dropped it, having severely burned his fingers. At this there was a shout, "He lied! he lied!" and the Goumbi man was declared innocent. I ventured to suggest that he also would burn his fingers if he touched the ring, but nobody seemed to consider this view of the subject.

CHAPTER XXXIV.

THE KOOLOO-KAMBA—THE GOUAMBA, OR MEAT-
HUNGER—EXPLORING THE FOREST—GORILLA-HUNTING—
WITHIN EIGHT YARDS OF A LARGE GORILLA—HE ROARS
WITH RAGE AND MARCHES UPON US.

We established ourselves in a deserted Bakalai village, a few miles from the banks of the Ovenga, and about ten miles above Obindji. I was glad that I had no olako to build.

There were with me several Bakalai; among whom, of course, were my good friends Querlaouen and Malaouen. Gambo was also one of our party.

After our camp was arranged we went out to look for gorilla tracks. It was too late to hunt; besides, we were too tired. In the evening Malaouen came in after dark, and said he had heard the cry of the kooloo, and knew where to find it in the morning.

Of course I asked what this kooloo was; for I had not the slightest idea of what he meant. I had never heard the name before. I received, in answer, a description of the animal, which threw me into the greatest excitement; for I saw this was most certainly a new species of ape, or man-like monkey; a new man of the woods, of which I had not even heard as yet. It was called kooloo-kamba by the Goumbi people from its cry or call, "kooloo," and the Commi word *kamba*, which means "speak." The Bakalai call it simply *koola*.

I scarce slept all night, with fidgeting over the morrow's prospects. The Bakalai said the kooloo-kamba was very rare here, and there was only a chance that we should find the one whose call had been heard.

At last the tedious night was gone. At the earliest streak of dawn I had my men up. We had fixed our guns the night before. All was ready, and we set out in two parties. My party had been walking through the forest about an hour, by a path which led, I knew not where, when suddenly I stepped into a file of bashikonay ants, whose fierce bites nearly made me scream. The little rascals were infuriated at my disturbance of their progress; and they held on to my legs, and to my trousers, till I picked them off. Of course I jumped nimbly out of the way of the great army of which they formed part, but I did not get off without some severe bites.

We had hardly got clear of the bashikonays, when my ears were saluted by the singular cry of the ape I was after. "Koola-kooloo, koola-kooloo," it said several times. Only Gambo and Malaouen were with me. Gambo and I raised our eyes, and saw, high up on a tree-branch, a large ape. It looked almost like a black hairy man. We both fired at once; and the next moment the poor beast fell with a heavy crash to the ground. I rushed up, anxious to see if indeed I had a new animal. I saw in a moment that it was neither a nshiego mbouvé, nor a common chimpanzee, nor a gorilla. Again I had a happy day. This kooloo-kamba was undoubtedly a new variety of chimpanzee.

We at once disembowelled the animal, which was a full-grown male. We found in his stomach nothing but berries, nuts, and fruits. He had no doubt just begun to take his breakfast.

This kooloo-kamba was four feet three inches high.

He was powerfully built, with strong and square shoulders. He had a very round head, with whiskers running quite round the face and below the chin. The face was round; the cheek-bones prominent; the cheeks sunken. The roundness of the head and the prominence of the cheek-bones were so great as to remind me of some of the heads of Indians or Chinamen. The hair was black and long on the arms, which, however, were partly bare. His ears were large, and shaped like those of a human being. Of its habits the people could tell me nothing, except that it was found more frequently in the far interior. I brought the skin of this kooloo-kamba to New York, and some years ago many people saw it.

On our return to Obindji we were overtaken by my good friend Querlaouen, who had shot a wild pig, of which the good fellow gave me half. The negroes feasted on the kooloo meat, which I could not touch. So the pig was welcome to me, as indeed it was to Quengueza, whom we found almost crying with an affection which is common in this part of Africa, and is called *gouamba*, but for which we happily have no name. Gouamba is the inordinate longing and craving of exhausted nature for meat. For days, and sometimes for weeks, a man does not get any meat at all, and whenever other food is brought before him, you will hear him say, looking at the food with disgust, "Gouamba," which means literally, "I am sick of food; I have a craving for meat; I care for nothing else."

I had some glorious gorilla-hunting while in the Bakalai country, in the upper regions of the Ovenga river. Malaouen, Querlaouen, Gambo, and I, often started out together, and remained for days in the thickest part of the forest. Now and then we would return to Obindji to get a supply of plantain, and then would go off again. We roamed over the forest in all directions; we explored some new regions; and sometimes we got lost in the midst of impenetrable mountains, where often for days we killed nothing.

In these excursions we suffered sometimes a good deal; for we had to endure many hardships. We often had very poor fare, and fever sometimes prostrated me.

One day, I remember well, we were out for gorillas; which we knew were to be found thereabouts, by the presence of a pulpy pear-shaped fruit, the *tondo*, of which the animal is very fond. I also am very fond of the subdued and grateful acid of this fruit, which is eaten by the negroes as well as by the gorilla.

We found everywhere gorilla marks, and so recent that we began to think the animals must be avoiding us. This was really the case, I believe, though I am not sure. At any rate, we beat the bush for two hours, before, at last, we found the game. Suddenly, an immense gorilla advanced out of the wood, straight towards us, and gave vent, as he came up, to a terrible howl of rage, as much as to say, "I am tired of being pursued, and will face you."

It was a lone male, the kind which are always most ferocious. This fellow made the woods resound with his roar, which is really an awful sound, resembling very much a rolling and muttering of distant thunder.

He was about twenty yards off when we first saw him. We at once gathered together; and I was about to take aim and bring him down where he stood, when Malaouen stopped me, saying in a whisper, "Not time yet."

We stood, therefore, in silence, gun in hand. The gorilla looked at us for a minute or so out of his evil grey eyes, then beat his breast with his gigantic arms—and what arms he had!—then he gave another howl of defiance and advanced upon us. How horrible he looked! I shall never forget it.

Again he stopped not more than fifteen yards away.

Still Malaouen said, "Not yet." Good gracious! what is to become of us, if our guns miss fire, or if we only wound the huge beast?

Again the gorilla made an advance upon us. Now he was not twelve yards off. I could see plainly his ferocious face. It was distorted with rage; his huge teeth were ground against each other, so that we could hear the sound; the skin of the forehead was drawn forward and back rapidly, which made his hair move up and down, and gave a truly devilish expression to the hideous face. Once more he gave out a roar, which seemed to shake the woods like thunder; I could really feel the earth trembling under my feet. The gorilla, looking us in the eyes, and beating his breast, advanced again.

"Don't fire too soon," said Malaouen; "if you do not kill him, he will kill you."

This time he came within eight yards of us before he stopped. I was breathing fast with excitement as I watched the huge beast.

Malaouen said only, "Steady," as the gorilla came up. When he stopped, Malaouen said, "Now!" And before he could utter the roar for which he was opening his mouth, three musket-balls were in his body. He fell dead, almost without a struggle.

He was a monstrous beast indeed, though not amongst the tallest. His height was five feet six inches. His arms had a spread of seven feet two inches. His broad brawny chest measured fifty inches round. The big toe of his foot measured five inches and three quarters in circumference. His arms seemed like immense bunches of muscle only; and his legs and claw-like feet were so well fitted for grabbing and holding that I could see how easy it was for the negroes to believe that these animals, when they conceal themselves in trees and watch for prey, can seize and pull up with their feet any living thing, leopard, ox, or man, that passes beneath.

The face of this gorilla was intensely black. The vast chest, which proved his great power, was bare, and covered with a parchment-like skin. His body was covered with grey hair.

While the animal approached us in its fierce way, walking on its hind legs and facing us as few animals dare face man, it really seemed to me to be a horrid likeness of man.

CHAPTER XXXV.

WE GO UP THE RIVER TO N'CALAI BOUMBA—A SEVERE ATTACK OF FEVER—THE TENDER CARE OF THE NATIVES FOR ME—ANGUILAI ACCUSES HIS PEOPLE OF BEWITCHING ME—I GO OUT AND QUIET HIM—A BOY CUT TO PIECES FOR WITCHCRAFT—A USEFUL IDOL—THE EBONY TREES.

With Quengueza I resumed the ascent of the river Ovenga. We were bound to the town of a chief named Anguilai. The place was called N'calai Boumba.

We left Obindji early in the morning. On the way we passed several Bakalai villages, the largest of which, Npopo, I afterwards visited. The river banks, all the way up, were densely wooded, but very sparsely inhabited by beasts. We saw no animals the whole day, except one monkey and a few birds.

Anguilai, who was one of the vassals of Quengueza, and a powerful Bakalai chief, and whom I had met at Obindji's, received us well.

Anguilai's town is the hottest place I ever saw in Africa. N'calai Boumba was set in a hollow, and the houses were so small and close as to be quite unendurable to me. The village was only a little more than a year old. The people had come lately from the interior. Plantations of plantain trees were very abundant.

Towards the end of April I was brought down to my bed with fever. This was the severest attack I had yet experienced in Africa. It entirely prostrated me. I looked like a corpse. Not a single particle of colour could be seen on my face. I had no strength. I could not eat. I could not walk.

For three days I had violent returns of the fever. The blood rushed to my head, and my mind wandered at times; so the natives told me. Of course I cannot remember what I said. I only know that my head burned like fire, and that I was almost mad with pain. Between the attacks of fever I really thought I should die and I commended my soul to God.

While I lay sick, people came and entreated me not to hunt so much and so constantly. They said, "Look at us; we hunt one day; we rest two. When we hunt three days, we rest for many days after it. But you go out every day."

I thought to myself, they are right, and I shall follow their rule hereafter. But it was hard to do so; for I felt that no one else was in the field; thatin such an unhealthy climate no one can live very long, and I wanted to do as much work as I could. I wanted to bring all the wonders of that part of the world to light; and I felt that I was getting older and older, and there was yet very much work to be done. So I prayed God to give me strength for the work that was entrusted to my hands.

I shall never forget the kindness of those native women to me while I was sick. Poor souls! they are sadly abused by their task-masters. They are the merest slaves. They have to do all the drudgery. They receive blows and ill-usage. And yet, at the sight of suffering, their hearts soften, just as women's hearts soften in our own more civilized lands. No sooner did sickness attack me than these kind souls came to nurse and take care of me. They sat by me to fan me; they brought more mats for my bed; they bathed my burning head with cold water; they got me refreshing fruit from the woods. At night, when I woke up from a feverish dream, I used to hear their voices, as they sat around in the darkness, pitying me and contriving ways to cure me.

When I think of these things I cannot help thanking God for them; that, wherever I have gone, He has made human hearts tender and kind to me; that, even under the black skin of the benighted and savage African, He has implanted something of His own compassionate love.

Anguilai and Quengueza were sadly alarmed at my illness. Anguilai accused his people of wickedly bewitching me. One still night he walked up and down the village, threatening, in a loud voice, to kill the sorcerers if he could only find them. I had to get up and tell Anguilai that I was sure his people and the Bakalai loved me too much to wish me to be sick. Whereupon they all shouted at once, "It is so; it is so."

After a few days I was able to walk again a little; and I went and lived in the forest, where I suffered less from the heat than in our little houses.

How sorry I often felt that these kind-hearted negroes were given to superstitions which led them to commit the most horrid cruelties. A little boy, about ten years old, had been accused of sorcery. On being examined, he confessed that he had made a witch. Thereupon the whole town seemed to be seized with the ferocity of devils. They took spears and knives, and actually cut the poor little fellow to pieces. I had been walking out, and returned just as the dreadful scene was over. I could not even make the wretched people feel shame at their bloody act. They were still frantic with rage at the thought that this little fellow had made a witch to kill some of them; and they were not quiet for some hours after.

I felt so badly that I went into the woods and took the path that led to the village of Npopo, which was not far distant from N'calai Boumba. I wanted to see if the men had returned; I wanted to see Aguailai, the chief. He was the doctor who had come to Goumbi to drive off the aniemba. When I went down to Npopo the first time I found the people all gone into the bush. Everything was open and exposed to thieves; chickens and goats were walking about; and I wondered to see such carelessness in the village. But in the centre, looking down on everything, stood the *mbuiti*, or god of Npopo, a copper-eyed divinity, who, I was informed, safely guarded everything. It seemed absurd; but I was assured that no one dared steal, and no one did steal, with the eyes of this mbuiti upon him.

This uncommonly useful idol was a rudely-shaped piece of ebony, about two feet high, with a man's face, the nose and eyes of copper, and the body covered with grass.

At last we started for the ebony woods. Our new location was about nine miles from the river, on the side of a long hill, and close by where a cool sparkling rivulet leaped from rock to rock down into the plain, making the pleasantest of music for me as I lay, weak and sick, in the camp. Five huge ebony trees lifted their crowned heads together in a little knot just above us. All around were pleasant and shady woods. It was a very pleasant camp, but proved to have one drawback—we nearly starved to death. I sent out the hunters immediately on our arrival. They were gone two days, but brought back nothing. Game was very scarce there; and, without an *ashinga*, or net, such as many Bakalai villages have, not much was to be got.

CHAPTER XXXVI.

HUNTING FOR FOOD—WE KILL A FEMALE NSHIEGO MBOUVÉ—A YOUNG NSHIEGO WITH A WHITE FACE—HE BECOMES MY PET TOMMY—HIS AFFECTION FOR ME—HIS STEALING PRANKS—TOMMY GETS DRUNK—HIS BEHAVIOUR AT MEALS—HIS SUDDEN DEATH—CONCLUSION.

At last I got better. I could not stand hunger and gouamba any longer, and determined to make up a regular hunting party and stay out till we got something to eat. Malaouen told me that if we went off about twenty miles we should come to a better game country. So we started in the direction he pointed out, and where he thought we should find the gorilla, or perhaps the nshiego mbouvé.

The men were covered with greegrees, or fetiches, and had cut their hands for luck. Anguilai told me that his *ogana* (idol) had told him that to-morrow the heart of the *otanga* (the white man) would be made glad, for we should kill game.

For some hours after we started we saw nothingbut old tracks of different wild beasts, and I began to think that Anguilai's ogana had been too sanguine. Finally towards twelve o'clock, when we were crossing a kind of high table-land, we heard the cry of a young animal, which we recognised to be a nshiego mbouvé. At once all my troubles left me. I no longer felt either sick or hungry.

We crawled through the bush as silently as possible, still hearing the baby-like cry. At last, coming out into a little place where there was very little under-growth, we saw something running along the ground towards where we stood concealed. We hardly dared to breathe, for fear of awakening the animal's suspicions. When it came nearer, we saw it was a female nshiego mbouvé, running on all-fours, with a young one clinging to her breast. She was eagerly eating some berries, while with one arm she supported her little one.

Querlaouen, who had the fairest chance, fired, and brought her down. She dropped without a struggle. The poor little one cried, "Hew! hew! hew!" and clung to the dead body, sucking her breasts, and burying his head there, in alarm at the report of the gun.

We hurried up in great glee to secure our capture. I cannot tell my surprise when I saw that the nshiego baby's face was as white as that of a white child.

I looked at the mother, but found her black as soot in the face. What did it mean?—the mother black, the child white! The little one was about a foot in height. One of the men threw a cloth over its head and secured it, till we could make it fast with a rope; for, though it was quite young, it could walk. The old one was of the bald-headed kind of which I had secured the first known specimen some months before.

A YOUNG NSHIEGO MBOUVÉ WITH A WHITE FACE.

I immediately ordered a return to the camp, which we reached towards evening. The little nshiego hadbeen all this time separated from its dead mother, and now, when it was put near her body, a most touching scene ensued. The little fellow ran instantly to her. Touching her on the face and breast, he saw evidently that some great change had happened. For a few minutes he caressed her, as though trying to coax her back to life. Then he seemed to lose all hope. His little eyes became very sad, and he broke out in a long, plaintive wail, "Ooee! ooee! ooee!" which made my heart ache for him. He looked quite forlorn, and as though he really felt his forsaken lot. All in the camp were touched at his sorrows, and the women especially were much moved.

All this time I stood wonderingly staring at the white face of the creature. It was really marvellous, and quite incomprehensible. A more strange and weird-looking animal I never saw.

While I stood here, up came two of my hunters, and began to laugh at me. "Look, Chaillie," said they, calling me by the name I am known by among them—"look at your friend. Every time we kill gorilla, you tell us look at your black friend, your first cousin. Now, you see, look at your white friend." Then came a roar of laughter at what they thought a tremendous joke.

"Look! he got straight hair, all same as you! See white face of your cousin from the bush! He is nearer to you than the gorilla is to us!"

Then they roared again.

"Gorilla no got woolly hair like me. This one straight hair like you."

"Yes," said I; "but when he gets old his face is black; and do you not see his nose, how flat it is, like yours?"

Whereat there was a louder roar than before.

The mother was old, to judge by her teeth, whichwere much worn; but she was quite black in the face; in fact, her skin was black. Like all the nshiego mbouvé, she was bald-headed.

Now I must give you an account of the little fellow who excited all this surprise and merriment. He lived five months, and became perfectly tame and docile. I called him "Tommy," to which name he soon began to answer.

Three days after his capture, he was quite tame. He then ate crackers out of my hands, devoured boiled rice and roasted plantain, and drank the milk of a goat. Two weeks after his capture, he was perfectly tamed, and no longer required to be tied up. He ran about the camp, and, when we went back to Obindji's town, he found his way about the village and into the huts just as though he had been raised there.

He had a great affection for me, and used to follow me about. When I sat down, he was not content till he had climbed upon me and hid his head in my breast. He was extremely fond of being petted and fondled, and would sit by the hour while anyone stroked his head and back.

He soon began to be a very great thief. When the people left their huts he would steal in and make off with their plantains or fish (for he could then eat anything). He watched very carefully till all had left a house, and it was difficult to catch him in the act. I flogged him several times, and indeed brought him to the conviction that it was *wrong* to steal; but he could never resist the temptation.

From me he stole constantly. He soon found out that my hut was the best supplied with ripe bananas and other fruit. He also discovered that the best time to steal from me was when I was asleep in the morning. At that time he used to crawl slowly and carefully on tip-toe towards my bed and look at my closedeyes. If he saw no movement, with an air of great relief he would go and pick up several ripe plantains. If I stirred in the least, he was off like a flash, and would presently re-enter for another inspection.

If my eyes were open when he came in on such a predatory trip, he would come directly to me, with an honest face, and would climb upon me and caress me; but I could easily detect an occasional wishful glance towards the bunch of plantains.

My hut had no door, but was closed with a mat. It was very funny to see Tommy gently raising one corner of this mat and popping his head in to see if I was asleep. Sometimes I feigned sleep, and then stirred, just as he was in the act of taking off his prize. Then he would drop everything and make off in the utmost consternation.

He kept the run of meal times, and was present at as many meals as possible; that is, he would go from my breakfast to half a dozen others, and beg sometimes at each. But he never missed my own breakfast and dinner, knowing by experience that he fared best there.

I had a kind of rude table made, on which my meals were served, in the open part of my house. This was too high for Tommy to see the dishes; so he used to come in before I sat down, when all was ready, and climb up on the pole that supported the roof. From here he would attentively survey every dish on the table, and having determined what to have, he would descend and sit down at my side. If I did not immediately pay attention to him he would begin to howl, "Hew! hew! hew!" louder and louder, till, for peace sake, his wants were satisfied. Of course I could not tell what he had chosen for dinner of my different dishes, and would offer him first one, then another, till the right one came. If he received what he did notwant he would throw it down on the ground with a little shriek of anger and a stamp of his foot, and begin to howl, and this was repeated till he was served to his liking. In short, he behaved very much like a spoiled child.

If I pleased him quickly, he thanked me by a kind of gentle murmur, like "hoohoo," and would hold out his hand to shake mine. He knew perfectly how to shake hands. He was very fond of boiled messes, particularly boiled fish, and was constantly picking the bones he found lying about the village. He wanted always to taste of my coffee, and when Macondai brought it would beg some of me in the most serious manner.

I made him a little pillow to sleep on, and he became very fond of it. After he was accustomed to it, he would never part with it, but dragged it after him wherever he went. If by any chance it was lost the whole camp knew it by his howls. Now and then, on some forest excursion, he would mislay it, and then I had to send people for it in order to stop his noise. At other times the people would hide it, just to tease him. He slept on it, coiled up in a little heap, and only relinquished it when I gave him permission to accompany me into the woods.

As he became more and more used to our ways, he grew more impatient of contradiction, and more fond of being caressed; and whenever he was thwarted, he would howl in his disagreeable way. Now and then I gave him a flogging to teach him better manners.

As the dry season came on it became colder, and Tommy began to wish for company when he slept, to keep him warm. The negroes would not have him for a companion, for he seemed too much like one of themselves. I did not like to have him in bed with me. So poor Tommy was reduced to misery, as heseemed to think nobody would have him. But soon I found that he waited till everybody was fast asleep at night, and then crawled in softly next some of his black friends, and slept there till the earliest dawn. Then he would get up and get away undiscovered. At other times he felt too warm and comfortable to get up, and was caught and beaten, but he always tried it again.

He showed an extraordinary fondness for strong drink. Whenever a negro had palm-wine Tommy was sure to know it. He had a decided taste for Scotch ale, of which I had a few bottles, and he even begged for brandy. Indeed, his last exploit was with a brandy bottle. One day, before going out to the hunt, I had carelessly left the bottle on my chest. The little rascal stole in and seized it; and being unable to get out the cork, in some way he broke the bottle. When I returned, after some hours' absence, I found my precious bottle broken in pieces! It was the last; and to an African traveller brandy is as indispensable as quinine. Master Tommy was coiled up on the floor amid the fragments, in a state of maudlin drunkenness. When he saw me he got up and tried to stagger up to me; but his legs tottered, and he fell down several times. His eyes had the glare of human drunkenness; his arms were extended in vain attempts to reach me; his voice came thick; in fact, he looked disgustingly and yet comically human. It was the maudlin and sentimental stage of human drunkenness very well represented. I had seen men looking exactly as Tommy did, and I wished these drunkards could have seen him; they might then, perhaps, have become so disgusted with themselves that they would have given up their horrid vice.

I gave him a severe thrashing, which seemed to sober the little toper somewhat; but nothing could cure him of his love for liquor.

He was also very fond of tea and coffee, but wanted both to be well sweetened. He could drink out of a cup. Sometimes, to tease him, I would not put in any sugar; then he would throw down the cup and begin to howl; and he would make the whole place resound with his noise.

He had a great deal of intelligence; and, if I had had leisure, I think I might have trained him to some kind of good behaviour, though I despaired of his thieving disposition. The older he grew, the greater thief he became.

He lived so long, and was growing so accustomed to civilized life, that I began to have great hopes of carrying him alive to America.

Sometimes he would come round the fire where my men were and warm himself with them. How comical he then looked! At other times, when they took their meals, and ate out of a common dish, Master Tommy would join the party; and when they would all put their hands into the dish, he would put his in also, and take a little handful of cooked and smoked fish. In fact, he kept time with them.

But alas! poor Tommy! One morning he refused his food, seemed downcast, and was very anxious to be petted and held in our arms. I got all kinds of forest berries for him, but he refused all. He did not seem to suffer, but he ate nothing; and next day, without a struggle, he died. Poor fellow! he seemed sorry to leave us. I was grieved; and even the negroes, though he had given them great trouble, were mournful at his death. He had hardly expired when the news spread through the village that little Tommy was no more. They all came to see him; he looked as if he were asleep.

It seemed as if we had lost a friend. We missed his mischief and noise; and for many days we allmourned for Tommy, and wished him back among us.

Tommy turned darker as he grew older. At the time of his death he was yellow rather than white. If he had lived to be old he would, no doubt, have become black, like his mother.

And now, young friends, for the present I have done. I have told you many things about Africa, about its strange animals, its terrible gorillas, its savage cannibals. And all that I have told you is true; for it is what I have seen with my own eyes.

But I have not told you all that I saw and heard in that far-distant country. I have many more singular sights to describe and queer adventures to recount to you.

So I will not bid you farewell: I will say to you "*Au revoir!*" That means "Good-bye till I come again."

THE END.

Milton Keynes UK
Ingram Content Group UK Ltd.
UKHW042145281024
450365UK00010B/618